"It has been suggested again that I should apply for a post at one of the progressive, that is to say, crank schools. I shall not apply for a post at a crank school. I shall remain at this education factory—where my duty lies. There needs be a leaven in the lump."

—*Miss Jean Brodie*

Old Students and Dead Princes

There's a moment when you just know it's over, and mine happened last week. I was sitting in the Jefferson Room at the Day's Inn on Route 144, staring at what looked like a spaghetti sauce stain on the speaker's lapel and just about to open my *Vogue* carefully, so no one would notice, when I suddenly remembered the opening paragraph of a senior paper entitled "How to Change The Oil In Your Camaro," by Travis Cray, a student in the first class I ever taught. The opening line was, "In this essay I am going to talk to you about how to change the oil in your Camaro." Professor Cray hated school, did not read, and could not write. He was a small-motor-repair guy and an amateur White Supremacist. (I say amateur because he didn't know what the word "supremacist" meant, but he wore a small enamel swastika on a chain with verve.) The paper was supposed to be five to seven pages typed, and in tortured, dysgraphic scrawl, he put his last gasp of patience and tolerance for academic nonsense into four wretched paragraphs with topic sentences like "First the engine." and "Then you twist it." His crankshaft logic was merciless; if you were too stupid to figure out the rotation of his thoughts then screw you—he just kept going.

Curiously, it was not Guiseppe Broccolo, the trombone playing, AP calculus whiz, whose name came back to me after all those years. Sure, I remember that kid, but Travis Cray popping up out of the blue was different. Travis Cray was a *visitation*. When his lame-ass senior paper popped into my head like a ghost from Classroom Past, I just knew it was time.

And this came to me while I was hiding in the back row of The Jefferson Room of the Day's Inn. Education conferences, by the way, are never at the Plaza. They are always at the Day's Inn, or a Garden Hilton, or—kiss of death—a Holiday Inn, in places like Malden and Methuen, Milford, Millbury or Millville. They take place in sterile, styrofoam environments with names like The Davinci Suite (a dump), The Franklin Room (water stains), and The Washington Room (carcinogenic). No place you can skip out and get some real Jersey Pizza, or even a good BLT. No place to buy a decent sweater. No place you would ever *want* to actually hang around and shoot the breeze.

Fluorescent lights and lukewarm, watery coffee make me queasy, so I'd sat in the back on purpose, just in case I felt like booking it half way through. I used to actually take notes at these things, but you reach a point in teaching where you know what works, and all the consultants can offer is perfunctory powerpoints and flow charts. The flow charts seem to point to an obvious thesis which the consultant takes two hours to explain but which would have been five minutes in normal speech, but you can never be sure, because there's always a technology glitch or a missing slide. Then the consultant wants you to talk about the flow charts at your table, and afterward she will call on you to "share," and she will write your contributions on a white lined pad similar to the one you used to read about Dick and Jane. She will praise you for being brave enough to be the spokesperson for your group, and no matter what asinine observation you state, she will thank you for it, and write it down on the giant sheet of lined paper. Then she'll fuss around with the computer for a few minutes and finally she will triumph with the missing slide, which consists of one misspelled conclusive phrase that is exactly where she was leading you all the time! You'll break for lunch, which is an indifferent pasta salad on limp lettuce leaves, bottled water and a chocolate chip cookie made from Crisco. When you come back, it's more fun with Dick and Jane, and finally 2:30 comes around and you all line up like cattle to be allowed to get your certification credits, because no one trusts you to just say you were there. I mean, they don't make doctors

3

do that, do they?

I am telling you, this kind of crap is enough to send you right over the edge. On the day I knew I was ready to quit teaching the presenter's name was—I kid you not—Valuable Cramson. (To get the ball rolling she told a soggy joke about how her sisters' names were Quality, Purity, and Charity. What a family.) While she talked I noticed that she had hands the size of footballs and her pretty scarf was covering up an adam's apple. She moved around ok, and she filled out her beige Banana Republic pant suit alright, but Val was definitely a woman-in-progress: a trans-Cram.

On this particular day, we were all going to experience the FishBowl structure. In this game three unlucky history teachers were asked to come up front and sit in three uncomfortable chairs all facing each other. The rest of us were instructed to move our chairs into a circle around them. Then, winking to the audience, sly puss, Val gave one of them an index card and said "Discuss!" then stood back dramatically, as if they might get some on her. She brought a pensive thumb under her chin and supported the elbow with her other arm, like a Carmen Miranda about to Chiquita Banana her way through the room. The three male teachers looked down at the card and after a moment the paunchy one stood up and read the card: "reconstruction."

Three history teachers, the goldfish in this scenario, were supposed to engage in a mind-blowing manifestation of intellectual prowess. We who sat around them—the bowl, I guess—were supposed to observe *how* they engaged. So I took notes: *The fat guy is starting to sweat,* I wrote. *The guy with khakis is really getting into this—he wants to show all of us that he knows the limitations of the Emancipation Proclamation, thank you very much. He also spits when he talks. The young guy is not saying much—he looks offended. By the crappy little chairs? By the khaki guy's spit?*

After a very long, uncomfortable discussion of the word "reconstruction", punctuated by very long, uncomfortable silences, Val stepped out of the shadows. "Now. What did you notice?" she asked, smiling inanely.

All of us bowls shifted in our seats. There is always a starter at these things, and it's usually a young teacher who is secretly hoping to lead her own workshop on Strategies for The Common Core, or Classrooms At Risk!

"There was no direction to the discussion…?" the teacher offered. Val was fiddling with the mini mike pinned to her lapel, but then she jerked her head up and smiled. The teacher tried again. "They just didn't have a focus...?"

"That's right!" Val is excited now. We have played into her giant hand. She scurries over to the whiteboard in the corner and we all scrape our chairs while she writes "lack of focus" on the board. "Good job," she praises the teacher.

Seriously?

Here's where it gets deep. Then Val asks, "*Why* do you think there was a lack of focus?"

Because all you wrote on the card was one word, you idiot.

"Because all you wrote on the card was one word," a young guy across the circle from me says. Val has to spin around to see him. We are soul mates, I think, except he is way too young for me. Probably a first year, I think. Jewish looking, nice cords. Needs a shave. Probably has a very sweet girlfriend he lives with. Maybe a cat. A Honda for sure, or a Kia. They probably go up to Bar Harbor for the weekend and have pretty good sex. Not great, but pretty good. I bet her parents are bummed that she fell for a teacher and not an investment banker...

Val swivels back to the white board, crouches and writes "one word on card."

Seriously? Does she have no original thoughts?

"So what's missing here?" she asks

smoothly, and she begins to walk slowly, pensively, behind us. She is enthralled with her own presentation.

"A goal?" someone else offers timidly. No one knows where the hell this is going.

"A goal?" Val echoes as she continues her slinky prowl. She's a cat circling its prey, a detective about to get the confession, a stripper about to swivel on the pole. With her freaking huge hands. *Is anyone else noticing that?*

We wait. And some of us more vulgar, impatient types think, *Where the focaccia are you going with this, Val? Is it time for lunch yet?*

Val is not going to tell us anything. She is going to make us guess until ten o'clock. We will be buried alive in the Jefferson Room of the Day's Inn on Route 144.

"There was no essential question," someone finally says.

"Good job!" she beams, rushing back to the whiteboard to write "essential question" on the board. "So what *is* an essential question?" she says, all thoughtful again. (People who don't teach love to define teacher words.)

"I think you just asked one," someone says with a chuckle. An appreciative groan from the bowl.

"It's like an essential understanding," says a woman next to me. More shifting, looking for a clock—Christ, why is there no clock in here? The whole setup reminds me of an EST conference, or a gathering of Pampered Chefs. They just keep needling you with inanity until you order a whisk or something. Until you cave and drink the Kool-Aid, then you can have your own Pampered Chef parties and torture your friends until *they* cave.

"No no," Val scolds. "They are different. But what *is* the difference…between an essential understanding, an essential question, and essential knowledge?" Val asks, pleased as punch. "We'll break for lunch, and afterward we'll talk about it." She beams. She actually thinks we have done some good work here.

People who don't teach are wild about the word "essential."

And right then is when Travis Cray popped into my head. I could see his Artic-Cat hat and his ferrety face saying, "Ms. Danner, can you believe this shit? You need to get outta here." Old Travis wouldn't stick around for a discussion of the difference between essential question, essential understanding, and essential knowledge, no siree. Old Travis suddenly seemed to me to be a man of substance. Yes, I thought, How to Change the Oil in Your Camaro was actually an ok title. Clean. To the point. I would read that essay and I wouldn't have to ask, what do we really mean by "change" the oil?

I was suddenly outside of myself, looking down at all these earnest teachers who were actually going to spend the afternoon mulling over these things, and I was no longer a part of this discussion, nor did I want to be. There was no anger or bitterness, and I certainly did not feel that I was over the hill or past my prime or anything like that. In fact, I was pretty sure at that moment that I was a good teacher, that I had been, at times, a *great* teacher, but that now I was ok with *not* being a teacher. It was just a readiness.

Weirdly, at the same moment Travis Cray appeared and I knew I was no longer a teacher, I had the most teachery moment of all. I suddenly remembered Hamlet, and how at the end of the play he knows he has to face his stepfather and he knows he'll probably die and he knows he doesn't have to keep up the exhausting game of pretending to be crazy anymore and he's just ok with the whole thing and he tells Horatio, "There is a special providence in the fall of a sparrow. If it be now, 'tis not to come; if it be not to come, it will be now; if it be not now, yet it will come. The readiness is all."

"That's right, Ham. The readiness is fucking all, man. Danner is outta here."

When you get to the end of your teaching

career, apparently you start to hear voices of old students and dead princes. It's like a parting gift. So I thought about Travis Cray and Hamlet for a moment, imagining them riding Travis's dirtbike and talkin' trash, then I gathered my stuff and walked out to the parking lot, got in my car and headed home. I was mildly surprised at my chutzpah but not really—this had been coming for a long time. I wasn't even upset about it. I was just suddenly certain that when this school year was up I wouldn't be coming back.

Now you—you're at the other end of the tunnel. I can see your tiny dark outline way down there, waving at me like the goober that you are. You're just out of grad school, all bright-eyed and eager, ready to go out and teach somebody something. You've got the degree, soon you'll get your first teaching job, and in September you'll drive your little teacher Toyota into the parking lot and you'll get out with a canvas tote bag that your mom gave you (monogrammed!) full of lesson plans from your portfolio and all your good intentions. You're going to be the best teacher in the world, Oprah will beg you to come to her school in Africa, your students will build shrines to you in the girls' bathroom, you will be asked by all your classes to speak at their graduations—but you will be cool about it, I mean, you will have to give others a chance—

that guy who directed *Freedom Writers* will discover you one day when he is conducting a nationwide search for the subject of his next film and he will choose you because he walked by your classroom and saw you surrounded by a sea of adoring lower-income kids, and when those kids are forty they'll still be talking about you at their reunions, and they'll *invite* you to their reunions, even though you will be too cool to actually go and anyway you will be having a sexy night in with your adoring, upper-middle-income husband, who thinks when you bite your pencil and one little wisp of hair falls out as you read over the next day's incredible lesson plan you are hot, hot, HOT. Even when you guys are going at it like rabbits, you'll be thinking up some relevant, real-world, multiple pathways to enlightenment for your kiddos, because you can't help it—you're Just. That. Good. You? You're going to *change lives.*

Yeah, yeah, yeah.

Assuming you didn't waste your time majoring in education, and assuming you're smart and young and talented and have a trust fund, you may bring something to the table, ok. But that's not what's going to help you *survive* your first year. And neither is what they taught you at Teach for America, or wherever else you became the delightfully misinformed optimist that you are. Five minutes in a real classroom and you'll be cursing those education professors up the wazoo. Even Nancy Atwell, winner of the Global Teacher Prize (and a million buckaroos) says if you're smart and creative you should *not* go into public school teaching. Seriously— there's so much working against you, and it can sabotage your first year and make you run screaming off to law school with a pack of rabid seventeen-year-old vigilantes in pursuit.

I've seen it happen. New teachers drop like flies, because this job is not for wimps. If you went into teaching because you love kids, go get pregnant, or start a daycare. Because teaching high school isn't about the kids—it's about the *ideas*. Real teachers don't care about the kids. The kids are just gravy.

But if you're in it for real—if you're *all* in— there are some things you need to know before you take your first class by the balls.

I know what you're thinking. You're thinking, what bitterness! What a burn out! I will never be like *you,* Maura Danner! And yet, blessed little Pollyanna that you are, you're still hanging on, waiting for me to give you the upside.

Well, of course there is one, and here it is: Teaching high school is mad fun, teachers have more power than the President of the United

States, and everyone else's job is boring as hell.

Screw Bloom's Taxonomy

First of all, there are three types of high school teachers. If you're committed to this path, you're either from a teaching family and it's in your blood (*"Gotta teach! Gotta teach! Go-tta Teeeeeach!"*); you majored in sustainability in college and now you want to give back, whether the world wants your organic arugula grown by Guatemalan orphans or not; or you are, like myself, an extremist. A kamikaze. A maverick. Someone who likes to teach because nothing is more important in this life than keeping the wheels of knowledge and insight turning in the right direction, prudence be damned. Teaching is a manifestation of character, people. It's moral fiber. It is knowing something about life. It is not for the faint of heart or well-intentioned. It is for the game-changing, dogmatic, over-the-top, the warped and the hard-ass. It is for people who know how to live.

That particular insight came to me fast and hard, so I never had time to think anything different. I learned it in graduate school, on my first day of student teaching tenth graders. My mentor teacher was Joan Finch, a sixty-ish lady with dyed, jet-black hair, horn-rimmed glasses,

14

and lipstick all over her face. (Did she not *see* it? Had there been an earthquake while she was applying it?) Mrs. Finch was old Boston Brahmin, she did not acknowledge the letter "r" and she ended every sentence with the word "dee-yah" like Kate Hepburn. She wore black slacks, sweater sets and little scarves to hide the creases in her neck. The middle-class thugs in the public high school where I was placed did not know what to make of her, because she represented breeding and culture—things they did not understand and therefore despised.

It was my first day on the job, and I was standing awkwardly at the back of the room, not sure of my role. I had met Mrs. Finch in the teacher's lounge just before class, where she told me abruptly that she had never taken on a student teacher before, and had no intention of giving up her power in the classroom. She didn't want me there, she'd been bullied into taking me on by the administration and she resented my uselessness. And let's be clear, student teachers *are* useless, even the good ones. So when we got to the classroom I intuitively backed into the corner, prepared to observe passively and dutifully learn from my better.

After the bell rang and the class had settled, Mrs. Finch approached me and told me discreetly to "Stop slouching, deeyah, and be the teacher." This was my first directive from on high, and I snapped my shoulders back like a soldier and stared at the twenty-four surly sophomores who were plodding their way through one of the dullest slabs of propaganda ever written, *The Grapes of Wrath,* with about as much interest as a cat has in interpretive dance. Mrs. Finch introduced me as Mrs. Danner and I panicked, thinking my mother had come to the school to check up on me. I smiled and corrected her with "It's Ms., actually." Her mouth froze into a strained curve of cracked fuchsia. "I'm not married," I said quickly, in case she thought I was being snarky. "Just livin' in sin," I added with a chuckle. The kids watched, bored with me already.

Mrs. Finch slid coolly behind her desk to observe me. Crap—*she's* a Mrs., I realized. She hates me, and now she's going to make me play Sink, which is Sink or Swim but without the second option.

I cleared my throat and tried to engage the class in a series of fishy, student-centered questions that I'd gotten out of my textbook, which specialized in fishy, student-centered questions. The "how did you feel about" kind of question. In grad school, long before Valuable Cramson and her fishbowl, they'd taught us that there should be an "essential question" for the kids to think about for the whole period or the rest of their lives or something, but with Old Joanie staring at me through her hornrims I went blank and could only spit out the lesser questions, with no connection between them. Nor could I recall whether the questions I was asking adequately reflected Bloom's Taxonomy, that prissy hierarchy of thinking skills, with comprehension at the bottom and evaluation at the top. Due to nerves, my wait time was non-existent, and so I was blasting nonsensical bullshit into the academic air like a popcorn popper gone berserk.

"What sort of symbolism do you recognize here? What does symbolism even really *mean*? I mean, do you see any at all? Can you find any ideas in the text? You guys must know what an idea is, right? If you just look at the topic sentence you must see an idea. I mean, Christ, you're sophomores, I mean—" Oops. I'd invoked the Lord. "I mean just look at the third word." I raced onward. "See it? Why do you think writers use words like that? It's not an accident. I mean, writers don't just cram stuff in there for the hell of it, you know. I used to *live* with a writer, so I know..." Oops. I said H-E-double hockey sticks. I swear like a sailor all the time, and when I'm nervous I swear like a drunken sailor, and dammit, it was going to be hard to stop. At that

17

moment teaching seemed arduous, artificial. My first insight was that I would have to change my whole personality every day for eight hours if I was going to pull this off. I hated this job. Correction—I sucked at this job.

I frantically tried another approach. "So let's find all the prepositions on page ninety-seven, ok? There's a whole lot of them in there..." I trailed off dismally. Grammar was my go-to if discussion wasn't working. I love grammar. Of course, I now know that I love grammar because I *understand* it. These kids didn't know a verb from a vivisection, which was what was happening to me right in front of them. No one said anything. "Wanna?" I added idiotically, hoping for a laugh. That's another thing I would have to stop, I thought—trying to crack myself up. Experience has taught me that teaching is *all* about cracking yourself up and having a great time doing it, but I was young, and trying to play by the book.

Mrs. Finch was making a unibrow at me. This was a nightmare. The kids were rolling their eyes at one another, and I was still up there, letting it all hang out and watching it droop on the line, when suddenly my mentor swooped out from behind her desk and bailed me out with hard-core content, which is what I should have started with. Screw Bloom's taxonomy and screw the essential question, people. That is lesson number one.

"Let's begin with the facts, shall we?" she said politely. "Tina, can you explain the phrase *caveat emptor*, deeyah?" Mrs. Finch's pencilled-in eyebrows zoomed upward toward her hairline. Tina, overweight, disenfranchised, squatted on her chair and said nothing. The class looked from Tina to Mrs. Finch's stiff, goaty pose, then back to Tina's sloth.

"Tina deeyah, can you answer me?"

Nothing.

"I'm talking to you, deeyah."

"Get off my back," Tina slurred, waving her arm out to the side as if to brush away a crotch-sniffing dog.

Then I witnessed it—the most extraordinary thing I've ever seen in teaching. In one moment, all hesitation was past, all floundering disappeared, the facade of academic banter dropped like a lead weight. Mrs. Finch walked up to the kid's desk, leaned over and put both her hands on it. She got right in that girl's personal space, and said in a low, throaty voice, "Go ahead. Take a swing."

My heart cranked into fifth gear and forty-eight eyes locked onto the scene. Tina turned her large head and stared at the opponent hovering over her.

Poker Joan didn't flinch. "Go ahead," she challenged, pointing at her jaw, "hit me." Her voice was like an anvil. It was the teacher version of Clint Eastwood's "Make my day". Apparently Mrs. Finch did not have a problem with squelching *her* true persona in front of the kids.

Tina squinted, pig-like, considering her options. "Don't tempt me, bitch," she grumbled.

Pause. There was a barely detectable narrowing behind the hornrims. "Go ahead. *I dare you,*" whispered Old Finch.

Nothing in my graduate seminars had prepared me for this. Blood would be shed, I was sure of that. And I would have to get into the middle of the two of them, one hand fending off the powerful arm of bovine Tina, who was easily three times my size, the other preventing my belligerent mentor from destroying both our careers. I could see the headline: *Teachers Gang Up on Student And Beat Her to Bloody Pulp For Not Knowing Meaning of Latin Phrase—Lawsuit Pending.*

I'd heard that I might have to break up a fight at some point, but I didn't think it would be between a *teacher* and a student. I took a half-hearted step forward with a vague notion of assisting, but it was already over. Tina had given the subtle but unmistakable sign of submission—

she had turned back around and put her chubby hands on the desk—and Madam Finch stood up like a stick pin again.

The rest of the class went like clockwork.

Back in the teachers' lounge I was still shaking when I told this formidable lady the extent to which her demonstration had made an impact on me. All I could say was, "That was extraordinary."

"Yes, deeyah, it certainly was." She was packing her briefcase, a battered black leather thing. One lump of frizzled black hair was boinging around her face. She seemed battle weary, resigned to the inherent struggle that was teaching.

"I mean, how did you know that kid wasn't going to pull a gun on you?" I asked when we made it to the parking lot. I was still shaking.

"I didn't, deeyah. One never knows."

"Then why did you..." I trailed off, not wanting to state the obvious, that she had chosen to provoke, heighten, exacerbate rather than diffuse. She had broken every rule of classroom management, yet somehow we both knew that if she hadn't, it would have been a disaster. With the foxiness of a card sharp, Finch knew that girl was bluffing. She knew what was at stake, and it had nothing to do with *caveat emptor.*

"Never be a wimp, deeyah" she said simply.

Words to live by.

I went home thinking she was a crank, but now that I've been teaching for a while myself, I'll tell you this. Old Lady Finch was the third kind of teacher. She knew something about teaching that goes beyond the rational or logical. She knew the truth, which is that kids are like horses. They can smell fear. They know what character looks like, and if you're short on the stuff you'd better fake it till you make it, because if you cave, you're dead. Be the third kind of teacher, people. Be a maverick.

In Truth or Dare, Always Take the Dare

Now then. Before we get into it, you're going to need a few pointers about how to get your first teaching job. I'm going to tell you how I got *my* first teaching job, and you are not going to believe me. You're going to think I made it up, but I swear to God, what I'm telling you is true. And even if it didn't happen to me, it happened to some teacher, somewhere. This, however, happened to me.

After getting my Masters of Art in Teaching (puh-lease don't confuse this with the even more imbecilic Masters in Education) which took me one hellish year and which, aside from the Joan Finch Method, taught me very little of value, at the age of twenty-seven I answered an ad in the paper for a schoolmarm in a rinky-dink coastal town just north enough of Boston to be officially "Nowhere".

It seemed like a daring and admirable thing to do at the time, quitting my low-paying editorial job at a magazine and escaping the big city rat race to start a new career as a high school teacher in a small town, where I knew no one and no one knew what a pathological liar I could be. I could see the sitcom potential here. I was going to get a cottage by the sea with wisteria dripping all over the place, and live a poetic life with my two-thousand-year-old cat Jukes. My best friend Claire would come up for the weekends and we would actually cook. Real food—no more take-out. We would buy lobster and get all crazy when the lobsters escaped from the bag and we'd try to swat them with a broom, like in *Annie Hall*, and the rest of the time I would enrich the lives of impoverished rural kids.

For the interview, I drove up the coast on a two-lane highway with occasional gruesome signs alerting me to the fact that at any moment a moose could lunge out of the woods, making me the 601st motorist killed by one that year, that the next exit was a good twenty miles away, and that there might be no more gas until Canada, so I had better stop HERE. I was starting to get a bad feeling, so I tried to call Claire on my cell.

No reception.

Jesus God.

I got off the highway and after a depressingly long, windy stretch of Jiffy Lube, Pizza Hut and several car dealerships, the road rose up like a wave and deposited me at a T-intersection. In front of me stood a caramel-colored stone church which apparently doubled as a movie theatre, because there was a little marquee on the side of it that said MRS. DOUBTFIRE 3:30 6:30 9:00 WORSHIP NOON DAILY. Small towns, I figured, had a charming way of combining limited resources. And in what universe, I wondered, did people have time to go to church at noon every day of the week? The light turned green and I turned right and drove past the town common, where two skuzzy looking teens played hacky sack, the dimmest of all the dim games. Kids in New York City had stopped playing that about five years earlier, I thought snobbishly, and I experienced that strange shiver that comes when you step into *The Andy Griffith Show.*

The high school entrance was a disheartening sight. It was an exercise in failed grandeur, with its excessively long driveway lined with naked, huddling little trees. Why are high school driveways always really long? Are they trying to hide the shabbiness of the buildings from the general public? The fact that the kids drool? It's like driving up to an insane asylum or a prison, I'm telling you. Halfway up the drive a chipped concrete slab announced that I had indeed arrived in Adolescentia. Some charmer had spraypainted "GET" in front of "HIGH", so I knew I was in the right place. The moronic fifteen-mile-an-hour speed limit seemed an apt metaphor for the teaching life, and I wondered what they were all doing back in the glamorous New York City world I had chosen to leave behind. Probably eating sushi and discussing Adam Gopnik's op-ed.

The American flag flapped in the wind as I parked the car in the visitor's spot and looked at my potential workplace. It was July, so there were no kids around, and the curb appeal was minimal. The building was a quirky blend of split level ranch meets Daughters of the American Revolution. The center building was two stories of brick and tasteful stone, but some wag of an architect had plunked on an unconvincing veranda with a sagging metal roof and rusty railing underneath it. A grim, corroded trailer jutted out from the right side of the building, and I imagined what it might be like to teach in *that*. Maybe they put the new teachers in there, I thought, where they huddle round the coal heater while the veteran teachers got to bask in the glow of the brick building and sip port by the fire.

My general impression? Here was a failing semi-rural school whose alumni probably smoked pot and rode around on dirt bikes in middle age. Weirdly, this assumption had a positive result. Provincial city slicker that I was, I had been expecting much worse—mud huts and a fenced-in yard where the kids picked lice off each other—and I felt myself relax. What the hell, I thought, and walked in.

A teaching interview is a cinch, if you know what to expect. Here's how it goes: There are several teachers sitting around a conference table. They have a list of questions they have to ask all the candidates. People in administration who have no contact with students and who will not actually work with the applicant have composed the questions, which they consider crucial, democratic, and lawsuit-proof. "Can you tell us a little about yourself" is always number one. Fair enough—they want to know if you can string sentences together coherently. They always want to know if you know when to shut up—a truly crucial skill in a job where one routinely holds audiences captive. The next question is usually "Describe your ideal classroom for us". Now you are supposed to avoid saying that you want the kids to sit in rows. Rows are bad, people. They smack of teacher-centeredness. Teacher-centeredness is bad. But the circle can be too cozy, too elementary school, and if there is one thing high school teachers loathe it's elementary school teachers *posing* as high school teachers. The semi-circle strikes a good balance and promotes discourse (never say conversation) and discipline (but say classroom management). What you and the kids really want, of course, is groovy corduroy couches with a cappuccino bar in the corner, but they never go for that, so skip it.

The subsequent questions are just formalities, because the interviewers have already made up their minds after question one, if you shut up at the right time. The lesser schools will keep up the pretense of interest all the way up to question ten ("Describe your philosophy of teaching") and then send you packing with vague promises and damp handshakes all around. If you've said anything remotely cynical, you're out. Conventionality is what they want in a new teacher, submissiveness and a willingness to coach debate. And even if it isn't what the interviewing committee wants, it's what the superintendent wants, and he or she will make the final choice anyway. (Superintendents always ask teachers to participate in the hiring committee, then they hire who they want and say that everyone had "input".) If you're applying to a more discerning school, they will see that you are intelligent enough not to fall for the debate ruse, so they plow through the questions and dismiss you with no promises, so they can criticize your dress and analyze the grammar mistakes you made in your cover letter.

NO ONE will ask you any questions connected to your discipline. Lesson plans, philosophy (how can you even *have* a philosophy of teaching until you've *done* it for ten years, for Chrissake?), your ideal classroom, "engaging the challenging student", yes, but if you are an English teacher no one will ask you to write anything, and if you are a math teacher, no one will put an equation on the board for you to solve. No one cares if you really know anything, so relax and play the game.

Now sometimes the interview may career suddenly off the path, and things can go terribly, terribly wrong. This happens when one of the staff has worked his tail off for about forty thousand years and this is technically his last day, since he has just found out that he is going to be ignominiously "encouraged" to retire over the summer, due to some little tramp complaining that he tried to look down her shirt, and he decides to lose it the day you come for your interview. What more can they do to him at this point, he figures. He then becomes the fly in the ointment, the hair in the interview soup. He becomes the Rogue Administrator.

The thing to do in this situation is to be *completely* candid. I know, I know, it sounds like madness, to actually tell the truth in a job interview, but this is the trick of it.

In my case, the Rogue Administrator was the soon-to-be-ex Assistant Principal, Mr. Mullens. I had made it through the initial round with the interview committee, and had made it past the science teachers, who were having a squirt gun fight in the hallway. Now I was in the Assistant Principal's office, for the executive chat. Roly-poly, myopic, diminutive, Mullens resembled the Mayor of Munchkin City. He practically disappeared into his enormous vinyl swivel chair. He looked like the kind of man who *would* try to see down a young girl's shirt, since he was not tall enough to see down a grown woman's shirt. He looked like the kind of man teenaged boys would make fun of, to his face.

For the first five minutes Mullens kept up a pretty good front of small talk and a couple of solid if predictable traps, until he clearly couldn't take it any more. After the familiar "How often would you communicate with parents?", he decided to throw out the list and go out on his own. I was halfway through lying about my brilliant and plagiarized lesson on metaphors when he crumpled the list of questions, leaned forward in his wobbly swivel chair and said, "Why do you *really* want to teach? Why would *you*," he put special emphasis on the pronoun for some pleasurable dramatic effect, "want to work in this *hellhole*?" He waved his sausage fingers through the air, indicating the presence of invisible flames.

Ruh-roh. That was weird. Not only had the tone shifted violently toward crude, but I sensed discontent. Subversion. Sarcasm rising.

Unlike most people, who find comfort in platitudes and saying things they don't mean, I find it stressful to fake it. The word "hellhole" shocked me, yes, but it also had the effect of releasing something, as if a finger had been removed from a dike. I said quickly, "Well, I don't really know...I just needed to get out of the city."

He cocked his dwarfish head at me with polite interest. "Hmmmm?" he encouraged.

"I needed to have different kinds of conversations, you know?" I figured this was a safe answer because, although appearing to be candid, it was actually only a prepositional phrase away from being a serious pedagogical opening. We could still go there, if he gave me the sign.

He nodded sagely and tipped back in his chair. I wondered if he was able to do that because he had his tiny feet on wooden blocks. "Most teachers are morons," he replied. "Can you take it?" he reached into a drawer and took out a small flask. He took a swig, then extended it to me. Truth, or dare.

Now this is what's known as a

professional crisis. The guy was obviously out the door, and intended to screw the Man one last time before he left. Was anyone recording this? Any hidden cameras in potted plants? The door was closed but it had a little window, and I could see an empty secretary's desk. Had she gone to lunch? Gone for more ice? Gone for the cops?

Like I said—this was a professional crisis. And what are you supposed to do in a crisis? Stay calm. Take stock. Look for the fastest way out. Except that's not what I do. So instead, I figured, what could they do to me? And anyway, I rationalized, I am way better when I'm a little loosened up. Every single one of my ex-boyfriends has said that. I also speak French better when I'm spliffed, who doesn't?

"Most people in *every* profession are morons," I said, then put the flask to my lips. I was unsure whether or not to wipe the top of it first, but it didn't seem appropriate, so I didn't. Ah, a nice smooth burn at the back of my throat. My brain started humming. Thank god it was vodka. No detectable scent.

People, I know what you're thinking. You're thinking, there is no way that I did that. But I did, because I could see that the man was on the edge. I didn't know then that it was his last day, that he'd been fired for drinking on the job and had been dragged through the ninth circle of litigation and was disgusted and bitter and that this would be his last act as an administrator or anything else for that matter, but I knew that I had to get him to give me the job before he went postal or something. Even if I didn't take it—the game was to get him to hire me. And besides, the part of me that has trouble faking it was enjoying this. If he had lit up a joint, I would have taken a drag. If he had offered me LSD, I would have contemplated Lucy in the Sky with him, purely for the narrative potential. No one would ever find out. I was behind closed doors in an office officially located in Nowhere, talking to a man whose reputation was officially mud. I can still smell the odor of What the Hell that hung in the air.

"How would *you*..." again the emphasis on the pronoun, "teach a severely autistic child in a Creative Writing class?" He said the last part fast, and his head jiggled. He wanted to be sure about me, so he was throwing one last dagger.

"Well sir, I don't think you can teach a *severely* autistic child Creative Writing. I mean, I could pretend I was communicating with him, but I'm not trained to work with that kind of disability, and frankly, if I *had* to give him a grade, I would probably be polite and give the kid a B." I probably should have talked about multiple pathways and alternative assessments, but I was riding the wave. Like I said, complete candor.

Mullens gave me a flinty smile.

"You're pretty smart. You're from New York," he said, as if those two sentences were part of a tautology. "Can you write?" He took another swig.

"I think so."

"Do you know what a coordinating conjunction is?"

"Yes." I actually wasn't sure, but what the hell.

"Can you *really* speak French, or did you just put that on your resume because you think no one will know the difference?"

"Yes and yes." I grinned. What the hell!

He threw his misshapen head back and laughed. Then he swung it back down and looked at me. He banged his pudgy fist on the desk like a baby Khrushchev and said, "You start on August 31. You're in the trailer. Dave will give you the tour. Good luck!"

I never saw him again.

And that, people, is how it's done.

The Good Teacher, The Bad Teacher, and How to Tell the Difference

High school teachers love to blame their lack of good results on middle school teachers, middle school teachers blame their problems on elementary school teachers, and elementary school teachers blame everything on the parents, which is probably the most accurate. The truth is that each level, of course, has great and small. The best teacher I ever had—and we're talking kindergarten to Masters—was my sixth-grade teacher, Mrs. Harris. Whaddaya know? A middle school teacher. My husband Charles swears that he is the mechanical engineer he is because of his fourth-grade science teacher. And we all know that a good kindergarten teacher is worth a hundred college professors.

As a new teacher, it's important that you surround yourself with great mentors. You're new, so you have no idea which teachers are artists and which ones are parasitic slobs. Here are a few obvious tells:

1) Never trust a teacher who won't let you walk into his classroom unannounced. He's either

embarrassingly unprofessional and afraid of discovery, or absolutely brilliant and doesn't want to share his expertise with *you*. Either way, this is not good. The culture of your school may not include open door policy, but a good school will always encourage teachers to observe each other. Even if everyone in your building is paranoid, just open your own door and invite them to watch you teach. It's not about being perfect, and God knows your male principal could and probably will walk through the door just as you are saying to the class, "All men are simple-minded, Molly. They can't help it." When I popped in on my friend Lucy, a music teacher, she was hovering over some papers on her desk, babbling to herself in an Irish brogue. I loved her the instant I heard her muttering "And I says to 'im, I says, oop yer boof with a rubber hufe, and go fook yerself while yer at it!" (It's a weird job, ok? And everything is funnier in a Scottish accent. Plus we talk all day long, so we're bound to say something stupid *some* time.)

2) Be skeptical of what kids say, but if *all* the kids say Mr. Jones keeps a cooler of beer under his desk, it's probably true. Don't repeat it—just take note of it. You haven't earned the right to gossip until you've been there longer.

3) A teacher who defends bad teaching practice

out of some perverse notion of loyalty to the profession is not who you want to be. So if the math teacher asks you to cover his class while he sneaks out on a Friday afternoon, say no. If another English teacher wants to borrow your test on *Macbeth* because she didn't bother to design her own damn test, say you're sorry, but you deleted it. Observe carefully—bad practice is usually attracted to bad practice. They sit together at lunch, and they want to know if you're one of them. So don't sit at that table.

4) On the other hand, in a staffing with an irate parent who feels comfortable letting fly with all the things you have done wrong because you are new and obviously incompetent, a good colleague will go out on a limb and say the following: "Now hold on here. Ms. Danner may have made a mistake, but she does not deserve the disrespect you are showing her. I've been teaching for three hundred years, and in her situation, I would have done exactly the same thing." This kind of loyalty is rare, but the colleague who has your back when some parent is looking for a scapegoat is a pearl indeed.

5) If you come ripping out of your classroom on the verge of tears because your dog died that morning and you couldn't get a sub and the principal yelled at you for missing bus duty even though you were at the vet's saying goodbye to

the best friend you have ever known and your lesson plan is a disaster and Lindsey Patterson just called you the C word and slammed the door which made your bookcase fall over and all the kids started laughing— a good teacher will pass by your room, notice that you are all blotchy and sniveling, and say, "I've got this. Take all the time you need. I'll cover your class." He will keep the kids occupied until the bell rings, and later he will stop by and give you a hug, then he will never mention it because he understands that it happens to everyone and therefore it does not need to be mentioned.

6) On Friday afternoon a really good colleague will ignore your pitiful "No, I'm OK, really" and insist that you join her for a drink because she gets that you are a new teacher and holding it together all day is exhausting and if you don't vent you will implode. You will spend an hour driving all over the place trying to find a student-parent- administrator-free zone so you can kvetch freely about students, parents, and administrators. You won't be able to find anything, and you will have to drive two towns away to The Bounty, which is the freaking Holiday Inn lounge out by the mall, complete with faux fishing net and plastic pirate skulls. People, if you have ever been to a Holiday Inn bar out by a B-grade mall you know what I'm

talking about. Only a true friend would take you to such a grim place and sit with a watery Tom Collins and listen to your boring old teacher talk at four in the afternoon.

Lucy had taught music in the trailer before I came, and she happened to walk by my door on her way to her car one day and saw me looking completely pathetic, as only a new teacher stuck in a trailer can look at the end of a horrible day. She and I ended up playing pool for a couple of hours that afternoon, yakking about kids we liked, administrators who were a pain in the ass, and whether or not the health teacher was mentally challenged or just faking it. I can't talk to Charles about teacher stuff, by the way—he gets bored. (And let's face it, I can only handle so much dish about thermodynamics.) Lucy and I find it endlessly fascinating, however, and you are going to need someone who will happily listen to you rehash your entire day, because only then will you be ready to go home and watch *Breaking Bad* without distraction.

7) Another sign of a good colleague is when she stops by the morning after the faculty meeting that you were supposed to attend but spaced on because you were too overwhelmed doing your job, and she tells you everything they said so you don't ask a dumbass question at the next faculty meeting. She will skip the boring parts

and focus on the highlights, like when the health teacher asked a dumbass question.

8) Finally, here is the real mark of a truly great colleague: As you are crying and venting at the end of the day, explaining how stupid the kids are because they didn't understand the implications of the Camille Paglia essay as it pertained to Woolf's novel, although you made it perfectly clear...she will put her hands on your shoulders and tell you that reading Camille Paglia with ninth graders is a mistake, you are way out of line, and that you need to redo your whole week's worth of lesson plans because they stink. This is probably going to be your best teacher friend, so hang on to this one.

Mullens was Right—Most Teachers *Are* Morons

Are you still with me? I'm sure you could get a decent score on the LSATs, if you decide to bail and go to law school like the rest of those wimps in your program, but I want you to hang in here. And if you're going to go through with this, you have to understand that you are, despite the great role models that you may occasionally meet, among fools. No—it's worse than that. Most teachers really are morons.

Before you get your hackles up because *you* are going to be a teacher, and you don't consider yourself a moron (does any moron?), hear me out. The truth about this business is that many people who would make great teachers leave the profession early in search of more rewards, and a lot of mediocre teachers hang on for years because no one ever looks in their classroom, or has the guts to point the finger at them. Or worse, after about two years they discover that teaching is too hard, so they become administrators. These are the worst. They got into the profession because they wanted July and August off. Or they wanted a job that would let them raise their family. Then the gut-crushing reality of what teaching is hit them and they bolted.

Thanks to incredibly low expectations, aside from the few Mrs. Harrises of the world, the ones who didn't become bumbling administrators are now your peers. Remember Debbie, the hillbilly girl who took child education in high school when you were in AP Euro? She's a teacher now. She can't write in cursive or understand the Constitution, but she's teaching the hell out of second grade somewhere. In a couple more years, she'll be teaching *your* kid. Yikes. Remember Jill from C lunch, the one who flunked woodshop twice before sleeping with the instructor and getting pregnant and dropping out? She's a teacher, too. Seventh grade. (She just *loves* kids.) The guy who makes the amazing margaritas at your favorite bar and deals a little pot on the side is dating a thirteen-year-old but his *day* job is teaching seventeen-year-olds history. No joke—these are your peers, and you must learn to work around them.

If they are not hillbillies, floozies or drug addicts, they could be vipers. Shall I tell you about Judith Enniger? The name Judith sounds a lot like *Judas,* but with a listhp, so you can imagine the role she has played in my life. Let me trace my own twisted path to collegiality for you. Should you find some sweet moral blossom in it, tweet it and warn your friends.

So there I was, twenty-seven years old and living a prematurely spinsterish life in a claustrophobic town where I had no friends. After a few weeks of raging against the lack of good cappuccino and the paucity of goat cheese, I decided to suck it up. It was in this spirit of lemonade making that I bought an old wooden racket at a tag sale and went to the high school tennis courts a few days before school started and met the antichrist.

I parked my bicycle and strolled over to the court, which was a grotty looking slab of deteriorating clay surrounded by pokeweed. I trotted onto the court and scoped out the scene. An active, older couple was playing at the far end, in the middle was a twelve-year old lump of a girl and what appeared to be her mother, coaching her enthusiastically. The wall was the only place left, so I slunk over there and started batting the ball against the concrete. After a while I found myself imagining the ball was my ex-boyfriend's head, and I must have lost track of what I was doing because the next thing I know I hear a voice say, "You might be a little more careful with that thing."

I turned, and there next to me was a tall, lanky race horse in human form. She had long, skinny legs swimming around in beige Bermuda shorts, and she wore pristine white Keds with pompoms peds. A crisp, white collared-shirt, a short, jaunty haircut, and behind the Jackie O's a fifty-ish, architecturally elegant face. She was rubbing her arm.

"Sorry," I said. She didn't do the usual female thing, which would have been to apologize all over the place for getting in my way, then five minutes later become my best friend.

"You're supposed to hit the ball, not massacre it," she said.

"I was thinking of my ex-boyfriend when I hit it." Maybe if I opened up she'd be nice. I'd been in town for one month, and I needed someone to be nice to me. The idea of massacre seemed to strike a chord with her, and she smiled. A little.

"I'm Judith Enniger," she said abruptly. "I teach AP Latin at the high school." She extended her wounded arm for me to shake her hand, or perhaps I was supposed to kiss it, because she let it droop a little. Later I would learn that people who teach AP anything always let you know it, the way Harvard grads always work that into the conversation within two seconds. People who don't teach AP say nothing, and hope that you *assume* that they teach AP. They'd really like to be teaching college, but for whatever reason they didn't, so they are obsessed with reminding the world that they are in fact teaching *at the college level.* This makes them feel like saints or something because they *could* be professors, but they just don't *feel* like it. High school teachers have inferiority complexes, I'm telling you.

"I'm Maura Danner. So do I." I beamed, all ready to have a sleepover and braid each other's hair.

"So do you teach Latin?" Enniger's voice was that of a person who had grown up with a maid.

"No. I teach English at the high school. I just got hired."

Something happened behind the Jackie O's, but I wasn't sure what. "No you did not," she said. My stomach moved a little to the left.

"Yes I did. I got hired in May."

"No you did not," she said, her mouth smiling at the sky in a demonic imitation of Ray Charles. I wondered suddenly if my little alcoholic transgression with Mullens had somehow leaked, making my contract void.

"Did too," I parried. We were hitting the heights as language teachers.

"Well, we'll see soon enough," she said, smirking as if she knew something I didn't. In the end, it turned out I knew something that she didn't. After five minutes I already knew what a

45

psycho bitch she was.

Ironically, the colleague who now hated my guts had been assigned to "mentor" me. This meant that she came into my trailer, watched me teach, scribbled things on a clipboard, then told me afterward that I would never make it. It wasn't my fault, she offered magnanimously, it's just that I wasn't, as she said, "classically trained." It was true, I hadn't majored in Geek at Miss Porter's. When I started teaching I didn't know much about working with kids, about the curriculum which had been lock-jawed in place for fifty years, or even much about the books I was teaching. I had read some of them, I understood the ones I read, and I adored a few of them, but I hadn't *taught* any of them yet. I was raw material, like you are now.

Enniger's favorite trick was making some obscure literary allusion in front of the kids and watching me choke. (With a smug chuckle and a wink at the class) "Ms. Danner, would you say the author is referring to Dedalus or *Stephen* Dedalus?"

Since I knew neither, I was forced to answer with a pedestrian "Uh...*Stephen* Dedalus?"

(Imitating playfulness but really reveling in the fact that I looked like a numbskull in front of my students) "Tsk, tsk, Ms. Danner! The author couldn't possibly have intended a Joycean reference, because that particular artist wasn't even a young man yet" (triumphant, supercilious, pun-smacking grin).

The thing is, a *really* smart person does not have to prove how smart she is in front of sixteen-year-olds. And a classy person who tosses out an allusion that no one understands is called a snob. Whenever anyone tries that crap on you, the correct response is to laugh and admit, "I have no idea what you're talking about."

But I was young and stupid, I fell for it, and now Enniger had something perversely picayune to say about me in her write-ups: No grasp of Joycean allusion.

If you're a young, talented new teacher, there is *always* someone like Judith Enniger out to get you. It's inevitable, because the whole system is essentially communist, built on mediocrity. You all make the same money no matter how smart you are or how high your kids' scores are; you will make exactly what the dumbest teacher in the school makes (less, if the dumb teacher has been allowed to be dumb longer than you've been there). This causes complacency among the staff, which in turn causes resentment when some hot young teacher like yourself ups the ante and makes everyone look bad.

My friend Jonathan taught fifth grade in a state which shall remain nameless, where it was actually illegal for him to teach above the level of the slowest kid in the class. Yes, there was actually a law that said he had to dumb down his classes (which, by the way, is the worst thing you can do for the "slow" kids, because they know they're slow, and this just insults them and makes the other kids despise them). So Jonathan, being the third kind of teacher, the game-changer, decides to teach the more advanced material at recess, for the more advanced kids. The principal gets wind of this, and puts the kibosh on that, saying Jonathan is not being democratic, he has to offer equal educational opportunity for all, etc. Ok, says Jonathan, he will teach *any* kid who wants to learn more during recess. So he does this, it's working great, the kids are learning quantum physics or something, then the parents of the other fifth grade teachers begin to complain because their kids are stuck with the lazy teachers who are only too happy to comply with the idiotic law and teach to the lowest level. So then the lazy teachers start to give Jonathan the cold shoulder because he's making them look bad. Finally, when it becomes clear that Jonathan is not going to back down, the principal comes into his room one day and tells him that he can go home, his classes will be taught by someone else that day. Jonathan knows he's being railroaded, but he has no choice, so he goes home and waits. The next day, the kids tell him that after he left, the principal asked the class if their teacher had any teacher's pets.

"Yes!" they cried. "Yes, he does! He does!"

The principal probably had a foxy little grin on when he said, "Who is it?"

And then something completely unexpected and wonderful happened. Every single kid raised his hand. "It's me!" they all yelled. "I'm Mr. Todd's favorite!"

Now this is high praise. Undisputable, spontaneous, guileless kid praise is the best kind of compliment. Because kids are no fools. They always say the right thing. Jonathan eventually left teaching to go save the Tenth World or something, but those bastards didn't drive him out. He left on his own terms.

Just remember, it's mediocrity and compliance they want. Your superintendent wants to make sure that you have never been a union rep, that you have no radical ideas about education, and that you will get the school's name in the paper for setting up a mentoring program with the local shelter and bringing the chess team to States. Young teachers do these things because they feel they need to be impressive, which is ludicrous really, because no one is watching them and there is of course no financial incentive for busting their butts, but by the time they find out that it is ludicrous, they've already done it.

The old dogs, like Enniger, become territorial. They are threatened by the young teachers, and can make them miserable. In order to avoid resentment, you have to tone it down, play it cool, lie low, and give the illusion of average. I'm not saying you should *be* average, because people, you must always, always be brilliant. Just do it on the QT from Enniger. Don't ever let her know how good you are, because she will hate you for it. Let her feel that she's the great and powerful Wizard of English, then shut the door and do whatever the hell you want.

I started my first teaching job with someone on staff already hating me because I had hit her in the arm with a tennis ball by accident. But I found out later that the real reason she hated me was because her best friend didn't get the junior English job; I did. Her old pal from the next town over had been trying to get into our department for years, but Mullens had kept her out due to some ancient feud about a paperclip or something.

I'm just saying, don't count on collegiality.

It's a myth.

Embrace Poverty

Oh yeah—another thing you shouldn't count on is making a living. You see, if you're smart and creative, there isn't much motivation to go into teaching because you can make more money doing just about anything else. Even working at a dog food factory. (Check out Purina's website—it's true.) You're going to have to swallow poverty, I'm afraid, unless you teach in Connecticut, and who wants to work there? Unless they're teachers too, or absurdly upbeat, your parents are worried about you. When you get your first teaching job and they ask you what the salary is, double it. No, triple it, then they won't ask again. Just look 'em right in the eye and say "Sixty-five thousand." Practice this before you go in there, because your dad just paid for your fancy-pants Master's Degree and he's all about getting his money's worth, which he won't, so lie. It's so much less stressful. I recommend lying to your friends, too, so you won't get the "Are you *kidding*?! How do you even *live* on that?" face at your college reunion. I hate that face.

Your students know this harsh economic truth, so don't worry about hiding it from them.

They learned it in elementary school. Remember that game, *Life?* You go around the board in adorable plastic cars and choose a career by picking a card, and if you get the teacher card, you get to pick again, because even Milton Bradley knew that you can't survive on a teacher salary, so you'll need a second job.

Still here? According to a dubious article in *Health Magazine* that I found on the internet when I should have been learning how our new grading program worked, teachers have one of the highest rates of depression. I just want you to know what you're in for, because the last town meeting I went to, they weren't arguing about how much to increase teacher pay. And they weren't talking about how to get rid of all the crappy teachers who make twice what you make, so they can entice you to stick around longer, either. So marry well, young one, marry well.

Whatever Gets You Through the First Night

I need to tell you about the dreams. Teacher dreams. When you first start teaching you'll be too busy all day to process anything, so at night your mind re-lives everything. You can never shut it off, the stuff just rattles around in your head. Conversations you had, conversations you should have had, the meeting that you spaced on because you were helping that kid with his essay, the brilliant insight about Emily Dickinson that you didn't get to but you have to remember to start with on Tuesday. If you're teaching six different groups of kids, you're going to have six different streams of consciousness running through your teacher brain from 11 pm to 5:30 am.

Worst of all is the night before you start your first day of your teaching career. To get through this, you will need a strong sleep aid and someone you can call in the middle of the night when the sleep aid doesn't work. Me, I had Claire.

"Hi, it's me. I just had a *horrible* dream."

"Yeah? Tell me your fascinating dream, Ms. Danner. Nothing is more fascinating than listening to other people's dreams, except having someone explain a Garfield cartoon. And I wasn't at all having great sex with my boyfriend, by the way."

"Shut up. It was really scary."

"Ok. I'm listening. Was it about school again?"

"Of course. I dreamed it was the first day and I was teaching *Huck Finn*. You know that's what I'm starting with, right?"

"Hey, did you know that according to Hemingway, all American literature comes from one book, *Huckleberry Finn*? I heard that somewhere."

"Shut up. Now listen. I'm standing in front of the class and I start looking at my notes, only there is nothing really written there. Just a couple of sentences that I can't even read. So I start talking about the river, the steamboat stuff, and suddenly I cannot think of a goddamned thing to say. I mean, nothing comes to me, and I have a feeling like it's all been said before and anything we talk about would be redundant."

"This is your idea of a nightmare—being redundant?"

"Well, yeah. It's horrible, to be in front of a class and realize that what you are about to teach them is trivial."

"God, Danner, you need to get a life."

"Shut up a minute, will you? It gets worse.

55

So there's nothing to say about the book and my whole hour and a half class is supposed to be based on a discussion of it. So there is nothing to say. They can't think of anything, I can't think of anything, so we're just sitting there. It's horrible. And I *know* I dreamed that because that witch Judith Enniger told me in our first mentor meeting last week that she didn't think the book was worth teaching. I *know* it. She said she'd always had trouble with it when she was teaching English, and now that she teaches AP Latin where the *real* literature is, she's so glad she doesn't have to worry about it...blah blah, Cicero, blah blah, Catullus. Barf."

"I will send her a kielbasa in the mail. Now back to your dream."

"So then I start trying to come up with something to say about Huck when I notice that my mouth feels funny, like there are little dry lumps in it. And so I sort of spit one out and look at it, and it's a tooth!"

"A tooth. Really. Are you sure it wasn't a Skittle?"

"Shut up. It's a tooth. And suddenly there are lots of them in my mouth, and I realize my teeth are coming out, and my whole mouth is gushy and gummy. Then I smell something funny and I put my hand up and my hair is on fire! I'm actually on *fire*, but just a little bit, and there's that acrid smell of burning hair..."

"Do the students notice that flames are coming out of your head and you're spitting teeth while stalling to think of something to say about *Huckleberry Finn*?"

"No, it's like the terribleness is *anticipating* that they'll notice."

"Ah. So the teacher's worst nightmare is really about the *possibility* of being redundant."

"Yes. Shut up. Now the worst thing that can happen happens. I look down, and I realize that I forgot to put on my pants that morning, and I am half naked. I am standing behind the podium, so they don't notice that I have no pants on, but I know they *will* notice."

"Again with the possibility of public humiliation."

"And here is the worst thing of all—are you ready?"

"Yes."

"I have my period, and I am gushing blood. We're talking geyser."

"Eew—that is just gross. End of session. See you next week."

"Claire, I'm a wreck. I am starting to think that there really isn't anything to say about *Huck Finn*, and I have to go in there tomorrow and be brilliant."

"That's just that bitch Enema talking.

She's getting to you. You *love* that book. You can talk about that book for days on end. You want to *marry* that book. "

    "Not the book, dumbass—the character."

    "Whatever. You'll be fine."

    "What if there really *isn't* anything to say? I mean, do we just move on to the next book? After three minutes? And what if no one will speak up in class?"

    "They'll speak. They won't shut up, I promise. Tell them that joke about George Bush and the parrot in the bar..."

    "I feel sick."

    "You're fine. You're just nervous."

    "There ought to be a manual for this fucking job. I feel sick. I should never have left New York. I've never felt this way about a job, ever."

    "That's because this job matters more. That's a good sign."

    "Shut up. Don't patronize me. Go to hell. I feel sick."

    "Ok, Danner, that's enough. You're getting abusive, so I'm going now. You need to have some Kahlua and milk and hit the sheets. I'll call you tomorrow and see how it went. Are you still there?"

    "Yes."

    "You were right to leave New York.

Everyone is totally self-absorbed and obsessed with cro-nuts. You're not missing anything. Really."

"Really?"

"Really. Now go teach the fuck out of Huck. They will *love* you, Danner."

"Ok. I'll call you."

"I know."

It's not always this bad. Around Christmas you will have a nightmare about not being prepared for the next semester because you're starting to get run down and you haven't even thought about those next books you'll be teaching. In February I always have a complete breakdown about not having seen real adults in six months and needing a really good haircut, so I usually have a dream about being bald. In June Claire informs me that I always have the same dream, the one where I get into a taxi in Rome, thinking I am off to cruise the Campo di Fiori and instead I get out of the taxi and there's my principal, the school psychologist, this horrible kid Jason Javronovich, his parents, and their lawyer, sitting at a café table, all waiting for me.

If Anyone Ever Says You Look Like a Teacher, Go Out Back and Shoot Yourself

If you are still there, you haven't quit yet, which is good news. The bad news is that I was up all last night, worrying about you. I don't know how else to say it: We are going to have to get you some clothes, or you're going to succumb to the dreaded and pervasive Teacher Frump.

I have a friend who interviewed at a swanky school and before she left she caught a glimpse below the desk and before she made it back to the car she had decided to change professions. She took one look at the feet and she knew that she would never be happy as a teacher. On the basis of teacher shoes. Teacher shoes are the first sign of encroaching Teacher Frump. They're chubby, stubby, and rubber soled. They're wide, formless husks that you put on your feet to keep you upright. The kind of shoes you can get at T.J. Maxx because no real store wants them, and by the way, that's where you'll be shopping unless you shack up with the computer programmer you've been dating. So until you have a joint bank account, you'll just have to go to a really *good* T.J. Maxx.

Do not wear anything called a "blazer." Or

"slacks", or anything with pleats. L.L. Bean jumpers are death. Your skirts should be more pencil than dirndl.

I know what you're thinking—you're thinking "As *if* I would ever wear a dirndl." But I'm telling you, if it isn't a dirndl it'll be something plaid, or stretch-and-go. Teacher Frump is a serious threat. After a few years, when you haven't seen an actual man for ages (and the men in your department don't count—more on that later) and you realize that no one but egocentric teenagers is ever going to see you, you will start to slide. It will be small things at first, like wearing tan pantyhose because your room is too cold to go bare-legged. Then you'll start to keep a teacher sweater on the back of your chair, a nice neutral beige or black that you can throw on over whatever you're wearing. You'll get away with it, so next you'll try that Thrift Shop Land's End shirt, (and Land's End really *is* the end) the one that doesn't quite fit around the boobs but the teacher sweater covers it, so you're good. Combine that with your wardrobe allowance of $2.50 a week and the fact that the only time you have to shop is when you are buying the huge bottle of Bean-O at Rite-Aid which you will need if you do not take my advice about lunch, and you'll cave pretty quick to the dirndl, my friend. Oh-ho-ho yes.

And for guys, it's worse because first of all, there are just fewer options for men. Secondly, really nice shoes and pants cost a lot of moola. Finally, you're a teacher, so you're not going to attract a lot of classy babes who could *help* you shop for pants and shoes then take you to lunch somewhere swanky. You're going to have to go shopping *with your mom.*

The truth is, teachers are the worst-dressed of all professionals, except perhaps plumbers. But at least everyone *expects* a plumber to look like a shlump. You wouldn't trust a plumber who showed up in Armani, right? The plumber is aware of this. So he cultivates his shlumpdom. And as the plumber must work on his crack, you must work on your teacher-look, because before the kids realize how brilliant and creative and fun you are, they see how stylish you are. They will work harder and get higher test scores if the teacher does not look like a teacher. This is a fact. Studies have been done.

Consider the case of Mrs. Fleabutt, the seventh-grade sub. Her name was tragic, yes, but even that could have been overlooked if it hadn't been for the dress, which was made from an armchair print and way too tight for anyone bearing such ironic nomenclature. Mrs. Fleabutt's actual butt was what we would have called gi-normous, and her massive upper arms had a seismic wobble that fascinated the class. The arms plunged down from cap sleeves too dainty to restrain such a force of flesh, and dangled over the papers she was correcting, or flapped in time to the words she wrote on the board. None of us ever read those words—we could not take our eyes off that appalling, pendulous jiggle. Mike Kakourous made up a dance that imitated its scope and motion which he performed in the lunchroom, and people, it haunts me still.

The hair is another area of concern. You know what I'm talking about—Mrs. Hayes and her bald spot. Mr. Jacques and his comb-over. Mrs. Brett's stringy little dun bun stuck like a wonton on the back of her head. These teachers were smart, they knew their content, they were always prepared, but they had hair that did not command respect, and as a result their classrooms went to hell on a handcart. It all could have been avoided with a good cut and some product, but they did not know what Mrs. Zeigler knew.

Ah, Mrs. Zeigler. It was 1968. I was in second grade. I was in a new school, and I was terrified. The first day of first grade I had spilled green paint on myself, hid in a stall in the girls' room crying and no one could find me for hours so when they did I was sent home in ignominy, and I was terrified that something similar would happen now. (All kids are like cows—they all think if something bad happened that one time it will happen again for sure. That's why they jump up and run out of the store screaming, or suddenly develop an aversion to shrimp.) Instead, a lovely young woman opened the door and welcomed me inside. I don't remember anything she ever said—but I remember how she looked. I must have stood there in shock before entering the classroom, because Mrs. Zeigler was a living Barbie. Tall, clear-eyed, she wore a simple tasteful shift, beige pumps and pearls. I loved her instantly—her long bare arms, her slender ankles—but her hair was lyrical. It was wonderfully poufy, flipped up at the end, luscious, long, head banded, Patty Duke hair. Most magical of all—it was not blonde, but *silver*. She couldn't have been more than 28 or 29, her face was so pretty and young, and the silver hair made her seem like a mermaid with shimmering, impossibly metallic tresses. I was so enamored of that mane I memorized the times table early, I read way more books than was required, I practiced my cursive during recess. That silver hair motivated me. If I could just get my hair to look like that, my life would be great.

Are you getting this? I can still recall my second-grade teacher's hair.

You are in front of the room all day. Kids are staring at you. Adolescents are shallow, judgmental, opinionated and heartless people, just like the rest of us. You've got about one minute to make a lasting impression. I recommend leopard skin pumps.

A Word About Craft

After the kids decide that you *look* like you might be an ok teacher, they will want there to be substance behind the J Crew Suit in super 120 Italian wool. What they expect is for you to know your content. So. A word about craft.

No one else will tell you this, so listen good, y'all. Your education degree probably did not ask you to know anything; the people who interview you, as I said before, won't ask you to write an essay or even give you a grammar test; that Praxis test you probably had to pass to become certified didn't expect much from you as a language technician, either. Weirdly, no one in this business ever wants to know if you really *know* anything. Even your college professors probably just wanted you to relate the novels you read to your own life, or perhaps, being too lofty to get down in the dirt with the writer and examine the language, they wanted you to talk about the "themes". I had a student teacher once who told me that all they talked about in her college literature classes was social justice, like if the protagonist was right or wrong, ideas of morality depicted in the book, etc. Now that kind of stuff might wash with a bunch of college kids who think the way to make the world better is to occupy the town common, but this is high school, people. This is *authentic* school; these kids want to learn *why* Gatsby is so great, and it's your job to show them.

This means you need to have an impeccable command of language. Which means how it works. Which means grammar. (Yes, I know I just plunked down two relative clauses instead of complete sentences, but I can do that because, well, I'm *me. And* I'm making a point. I know the rules, and dammit, I know when I'm breakin' 'em!) That same student teacher who knew all about whether *Moll Flanders* was literary art or moral imperative could not find the proper nouns in Defoe's title. "We never talked about the actual *writing* in my college classes," she told me. Poor kid, she was smart and talented, but had crappy craft. It's not her fault; she went to a very swanky liberal arts college where everyone drives a Prius but nobody learns anything about writing.

It happens a lot. Young Folk who want to teach English often don't know shit about English. Imagine applying for a job as a chemist without knowing the periodic table, or a history teacher not knowing the actual date of the American Revolution. Tables, dates, forms are important. Besides, you're the teacher, and the kids want to see that you've worked to master your content, kiddo. You need to acquire a patina. How do you think Dumbledore commanded so much respect? Do you really think he didn't know that "Expecto Patronum" is not an imperative, but a first conjugation verb expressed in the first person followed by a second declension masculine noun in the accusative? And by the way, one secret to Fitzgerald's masterpiece is in the first six paragraphs of Chapter 3, in the sequence of verb tenses, which you can only spot if you're looking at the verbs. But first you have to know what a verb is.

Your first assignment, then, before you set foot in a classroom as a teacher of writing and literature, is to cultivate your command of grammar. Don't make that face, and don't listen to anyone who says it's irrelevant, unnecessary or boring. Consult your George Orwell and repeat after me: Grammar is sexy.

That said, it is also true that some grammar is indeed pointless, and a good English teacher knows the difference. There is no need for anyone to understand that a prepositional phrase can function as an adverb. I am not suggesting that you use the odious *Warriner's Grammar* in the classroom, but I am telling you to use the odious *Warriner's Grammar* to teach yourself, so you can then teach grammar much more effectively to the kids. If you sidestep this you are cheating your students—and yourself—out of a real language education. Besides, kids love to look for mistakes in reputed masterpieces, and when smartass Jasmine Muratta asks you if that is indeed a dangling modifier in the second paragraph of chapter five in *The Scarlet Letter* you're going to have to say no, young one, Hawthorne knew exactly what he was doing. That participle is actually modifying the previous antecedent, which is of course separated by multiple relative and subordinate clauses, because Hawthorne loves a good periodic sentence—who doesn't? Then make her write an imitation of that beautiful, ornate sentence and go over it with her, one grammatical chunk at a time, so she can really understand why it's so elegant. Don't let her get away with skipping a single clause or phrase. She'll come out of your room saying how she has never written a sentence like that in her whole life. She'll have a new appreciation for Hawthorne's art and for her English teacher. See? *Patina.*

You must also know the books you're going to be teaching. Obviously, as a new teacher you don't know jack shit, because you come to know the books by *teaching* the books.

So admit that you don't know shit, and re-read the books every night with the kids, and take copious notes. Trust your own reading and have a point of view about every book you teach. The kids expect you to have a take on the book; they don't want you to leave it up to them to figure it out, so please don't ask them to write a journal entry about what *they* would do if *they* were in the protagonist's shoes. And Jesus God, don't ask them to write a blog about it. If you teach them right, these books will be the best friends you ever have. These books will be the last words on their dying lips. These books will make them better people. These books will save their souls if they ever end up in a P.O.W. camp, which looks more and more possible these days, especially with Trump in office. The books, kiddo. You are in it for the books.

Do not, under any circumstances, use a teacher's guide. These are *SparkNotes* for incompetent educators. Enough said.

You're an English Teacher: Do the Math

All young English teachers hear apocryphal tales of never-ending papers to grade from veterans who love to brag about how they spend hours each night correcting kids' papers. They think this makes them good teachers, dedicated teachers, but it's actually a dead giveaway that they are inefficient teachers.

Most teachers are so hyper about producing grades that they forget to actually teach writing. They forget that writing instruction is all in the pre-grade strategy.

If you're good, by the time you're ready to evaluate their papers you have already let your students talk with you and each other about their papers. There may have been some slap-dash outlining and paragraph mapping, or you might have all written a first paragraph together then looked at them and offered suggestions. You have already taught them how to introduce and punctuate a quote, or how to avoid repetition in a conclusion. They've probably had a chance to write an observation of another kid's paper, so they can see how other kids approach the assignment, and they can practice noticing things about writing. They've written at least two drafts of their so-called paper before it ever gets to your little red pen.

Most importantly, you've shown them models of good writing, and they all have annotated copies of those models in their notebooks.

Modelling is especially crucial when it comes to literary analysis, probably the most useless form of writing and yet the one everyone wants the kids to know how to produce, even if their life plan is to open a food truck that sells deep-fried popsicles. And think about it: No one with any kind of a life ever sits around reading literary criticism. No respectable potty has as its companion *A Question of Credibility: The Subjective Narrator of Dostoevsky's Notes from Underground.* The kids have literally never encountered this animal, and then they hit high school and blam! Everyone's smoking pot and writing essays on subjective narration. If it were up to me, I would skip the analysis and get them to write a sonnet, but the world still loves an AP prompt, so you have to find some palatable examples of this and break it down for your students.

I know what you're thinking: This drafting and revising stuff sounds great, but kids won't put any effort into anything unless they know you're grading it. They'll show up with it half done, or not done at all, or they say they did it but really they cut and pasted a paragraph over and over so it *looks* like two pages. Remember, kids are essentially evil. Even the nice ones. So you really do need to look at all these pieces yourself.

Did you hear what I said? I said *look* at them, not grade them. But you are going to fake them out by telling them that you are going to *collect* their drafts. Be official—have the folder that you're going to put the papers into right in your hand as you say this. Tell them up front that you are not grading these first efforts, but you are going to *look* at them because you want to see what they've done so far. You are going to collect them and look at them at the end of the class, and again when they submit their final drafts, and you expect to see a lot of changes from the first draft. Then collect them, look at them—but don't write anything on them. Or write one little remark next to one paragraph, so they know you mean business. These first efforts are a little snapshot of how the class is doing overall, who might need some help next class, that sort of thing. So collect the papers every single class, look them over, pass them out the next class, and let the kids do their work. Collect and look at everything, but grade only the final and best writing.

Once your students have gone through the process of drafting and revising, and you are ready to evaluate their drivel, here's how to approach it: Figure you have five classes. Each class has twenty-five kids (if you're lucky). When you think about the craft of writing, and how complex it is, it's reasonable to figure they should write at least one paper a week. (Two or three, actually, but you would have to take a lot of amphetamines to pull this off.) This means you will have 125 papers a week to grade. Thoughtful correcting requires long stretches of quiet, so you can concentrate on what the heck the kid is trying to say, so getting anything done at school is ludicrous. Your union-contracted prep period is constantly eroded by IEP meetings, kids who need help, waiting for the Xerox machine which is always broken, hauling ass across the parking lot to the ladies' room and—guess what?—preparing for your next class.

So there you are, with 125 papers a week if you're a decent writing teacher. Figure each paper takes, conservatively, five minutes to look at, but ten once you've stopped to mark it up. Think about it. Ten minutes is not that long to evaluate a two-page paper; you probably should be spending a lot more time on each one, writing a long personal note so the kid can really improve. That's 1250 minutes a week, or 20.8 hours. *That's four extra hours a day.* As if you could even stand to *do* it that long. I would, as Claire would say, rather shave my legs with a cheese grater.

Which brings me to the state of mind you must be in to correct these things. You can't just sit down and bash off a few, then go shopping, then make dinner, then watch the news and then go do a couple more. If you want to do this right, you need to be in the same mindset from the first essay to the last crappy conclusion of the very last paper in the pile. You have to hold in your head the focus of the assignment, the criteria you've established. If you don't do this, and instead you go out and have a few drinks with Claire, or watch *Sherlock* in between papers, you will be tired, or bored, or irritated and you'll just want to get through them, so the poor suckers whose papers are last get hasty C's, while the first careful few have higher marks because you had more energy and compassion and patience when you first sat down.

But who has four hours of uninterrupted time a day to correct papers, or do anything for that matter? I can't even unlock the door to my classroom without someone bugging me to do something.

Many an English teacher burns out

because of this. You, however, will not, because you have me.

First of all, you never assign a two-page paper. Assign a one-page paper, single-spaced. It's the same amount of words, but you would be shocked at the psychological difference it makes when you grab your coffee and sit down to task. And one page single-spaced is enough for most young writers to introduce, develop and finish an idea. It's the craft you want to teach them, remember, not how to extend an already shaky thesis into two thin pages. If the paper is all crushed onto one page, your eyes can then take in the whole shaboom more easily. That is, you can see the whole paper at once, and you can evaluate it more efficiently—perhaps in seven minutes, rather than ten. So you've just cut your correcting time to 2.9 hours a night. And don't worry—when it comes time to write the five or ten-page paper, which of course they must also tackle, they will have good habits under their belt *because you've made them write so much.*

Secondly, keep your criteria simple. Decide straight off that this paper is all about the topic sentences, and how they connect. Or maybe it's about the conclusion, or getting them to have an opener a little more creative than "In this essay I am going to talk to you about how to change the oil in your car." No more than three objectives, then look only for those objectives, and comment only on those three objectives. You let a lot of other stuff go, but you can focus on that stuff in the next assignment. Remember, the trade-off is they will be writing a lot and they'll improve with practice. Most new teachers spend hours writing little encouraging notes to the kids, who spent less time writing the damned thing. This is all about getting them to work harder than you do.

Thirdly, circle mistakes, never, never correct them. That's *their* job. And I wouldn't even circle the mistakes if you are not going to require a revision. They won't even look at the marks you make if they know that's the final grade. You shave off at least three minutes per paper doing this. So now you're down to 1.7 hours a night.

If the first paragraph is incoherent, stop reading the paper, write incoherent on the top of the page, indicate with a slash exactly where you stopped reading, give it an F, and go to the next one. This could cut a lot of time off, depending on the class. You're probably down to one hour now.

Ah, yes. That's so mean.

Well, yes, it is. Guess what, folks: good teaching implies high standards. You model it, you explain it, you let them hash it out in discussion, they write a quick draft in class and you read a few out loud and critique the points of focus, then they go home to write the paper and you can expect something of them. I tell my students that serving up sloppy prose is the equivalent of inviting someone to dinner, then slapping down a box of Lucky Charms because you didn't feel like cooking, then expecting them to rave about it. Thirdly, always allow a revise, IF the student comes and conferences with you first. This will weed out any grade grubbing, entitled types who only want to nag you into giving them the A they think they deserve. This describes most kids who complain about their grade. There are usually three or four, maybe five students per assignment who are actually willing to take the time to have a conversation about their writing. This is one-on-one, differentiated instruction, by the way, and you are offering it to the whole class because you are an excellent teacher.

Finally, and this is important, never ever grade something turned in late. You're on a tight schedule here. This is not because you're in a frantic rush, although of course you are, but because there is so much great stuff to teach and you want to make sure you have the time to go deep into what needs to be gone into deeply. It's blinking difficult to maneuver twenty-five kids through a complex piece of literature, and the kids need to stay with you for it all to work. If they are turning in work late, the party's been over for a long time, and the champagne is flat, and you are no longer in the party mood. A late essay gets an automatic 50. You don't have to read it—you don't want to reinforce negative behavior with a lot of attention.

Just eyeball it, see that the assignment was done (as opposed to the old repeating paragraph trick) and slap a 50 on it. Do this consistently and this will shock and outrage the students who always turn things in late, and will deeply satisfy the ones who get it in on time, which is exactly what you want.

There is a lot of current pedagogy coming at you that will tell you that giving a late grade is not a good idea—that holding students accountable is bad for kids, that in the real world, people are not penalized for being late. (Really? No consequences? Just miss your first class because you went out for coffee and gosh—just lost track of the time—then see if there are not consequences.) The fact that there are 25 of THEM and only one of YOU should be enough to convince anyone that a moving deadline is not a reasonable idea. The student should never be at the center of the universe, unless you want to produce a generation of people who think the universe revolves around them. Instead, teach the kids to revolve around reasonable deadlines, so you can do your job without feeling like they are the customer and you are the waitress.

Assign lots of one-page papers, have a pre-grade strategy, keep your criterion simple, never write corrections on a paper, allow a revise with conference, and never grade a late paper. You'll have an hour a day of correcting, but you can even do it at school, if you can find a hiding place. I use the janitor's closet on the second floor. No one bothers me, and I'm out of there for cocktails at four.

Go to the Ladies' Room Before the Bell Rings

Teaching high school is like living in Seattle. Everyone who lives in Seattle knows that the rain is not a big deal, but everyone who doesn't live there thinks it's always cold, wet and miserable. When I tell people that I teach high school most people say something like "Wow, you've got guts", or "Huh. That's a challenge." Ironically, as they proudly tell me what *they* do for a living, I am thinking to myself, *Human Resources, really? Wow.*

There is no time to be bored in this job. Here, *en bref,* is what a typical day of first year teaching looked like for me:

7:00: Terrence is squatting by my trailer door. He's been there since 6:30, waiting for me to explain to him why everyone's all over John, Paul and George, but no one really appreciates Ringo. It's a worthy question, so I invite him in and we chat about it as I hang up my coat and drink my coffee. Then Mallory shows up with her blue hair and her latest poem, which is really, really good. *New Yorker* good. I think about stealing it, but instead I put it on my desk with scotch tape so I can read it whenever I hate my students. She doesn't get along with Terrence—

no one does—so he leaves pretty quick.

7:45: The room is starting to buzz with my first period class. Here is something very few people know about high school kids: they're affectionate as hell. They come up and sit on the edge of my desk, or they stand on the other side of it and sort of shift their feet like expectant dogs while they talk, or they crowd around me as I'm trying to get to the table to lay out some papers. I ask them to please stop fiddling with my stapler, and they don't get mad, because they think I'm kidding, even though I'm not. The best thing is you can yell at them and, like dogs, they just take it. They still stand there, wagging their tails and looking at you. They're sure you don't really mean it when you yell, and *you* know that you *do* mean it but you pretend to like them because it's easier so they keep wagging their tails and then you actually start to like them but they think you still want to pretend that you don't, so they keep pretending to annoy you and you pretend to be annoyed but secretly you LOVE them now and hope that they don't know it because if they know it you are toast, and of course they have known it all along, but *you* didn't, so it's all good.

At 7:58, I see Zachary in the back of his room, on his phone.

"Zachary! Give me that cell phone, now."

"I'm talking to my mom."

"Good. I'd like to tell her about our cell phone policy. Gimme the phone."

"Oh my God, you are so uptight." (Relinquishing the phone.)

"Yes, I am indeed uptight."

"Hey, have you ever heard a band called Ninth Rail?"

"No."

"They're really good. You'd like them."

"Great. Now stop touching my stapler."

(Releasing the stapler) "Seriously. Check it out. I'll send you the link."

(Said without enthusiasm) "Yay. Now get out."

(Huge boy-smile)

At 8:00 the bell rings, we are off and running. I give the kids the homework right away, then we analyze a sentence or two, play a fabulous interesting and educationally dynamic review game, probe a deep philosophical question or two, linger over a particularly lovely passage, discuss the use of the subjunctive in the first line and start work on an imitation exercise.

9:30: Lunch. Yes, lunch. No surprise, since breakfast was at 5:30 am, four hours ago. Man, I am freaking starving, and I have twenty minutes to refuel. Fifteen by the time I get rid of

Zachary. Ten if I count the Xeroxing for my next class. But who's counting? Let me tell you, at this job you will learn to choke down food like a sumo wrestler in a hot dog eating contest. When you know you're not going to eat again for six hours, you eat. You may actually lose weight in this profession, because you are always on your feet and sometimes you don't even get lunch. There is a trick to it, though. Always bring your lunch, and make sure it's not soup. You cannot chug soup. It should be served cold—you can piss your whole lunch away waiting for the microwave. Potato chips are fine, popsicles take too long. Salads work pretty well, if they don't wilt. Of course, if you eat it at 9:30 you should be ok. PB&J is quick and cheap (remember, you will be broke), but humiliating. Personally, I like cold leftover pizza, but that's up to you. Do not, repeat, do NOT eat anything from the cafeteria. And I might take a moment to mention that you may have to deal with the horror, the horror of eating lunch to the sound of people flushing the toilet. Yes, it's true—there are schools where the faculty restroom is actually in the teachers' lounge, or even worse—in the cafeteria. In that case, you will want to eat lunch in your room. Enough said.

10:45: Amanda has her scheduled break down and storms out of the class, furious because I wouldn't let her do her nails while the other kids were presenting. I shout after her, "I've enjoyed our talk!" and the kids laugh.

11:30: There is a knock at my door, and I see a pudgy, frantic kid gesturing for me to come out there and talk to him. I go out and he tells me that he's pretty sure my car has mysteriously started itself and rolled into the ditch in the back parking lot. His whole French class saw it, because their classroom faces the back parking lot. Mrs. Duncan tried to stop him from looking out the window until he told her, then she told him it was my car and to run and get me. So now I have to take all my students outside because you can't leave them alone in the room for a nanosecond in case someone goes into anaphylactic shock or something and you're not there to stab him with the epi pen (like I'm really going to do *that*—I faint at the sight of nail clippings). So we all put on our coats and walk out into the back parking lot to share in my humiliation and sure enough, my little Ford Escort's butt is hanging out of the ditch. I know what happened, of course, because I always forget to pull the emergency brake hard enough. I'm usually in such a mad rush to get to school, and I'm thinking about too many things, and I was trying to follow that story about the Israeli sniper on NPR, and I just didn't use the brake, and the gears are kind of loose, and I guess there actually is a slight incline at the back of the lot.

"I bet Amanda will be sorry she missed this," Tyler points out, and we all agree. I dial my Triple A and arrange for the pickup, then we trudge back into class. It's actually kind of nice to be outside. There are trees, I notice.

12:30: I am brilliant, amazing, stunning in my ability to multi-task. I am taking apart Act 3 of Hamlet while operating my Smartboard which always malfunctions just when I need it and I am keeping an eye on the clock but also watching Molly and Haley in the back because they chat all the time and you already know Zachary who has ADD (everyone named Zachary has ADD) and needs to get up spontaneously and move around and at the same time I need to address the uncompromising stare coming from Ben in the front row, who is not convinced that I am smarter than he is, and I of course have to remember that there is a fire drill scheduled for any moment and I will have to get Sharon Kaminsky out of the trailer in her wheelchair and I can't forget to go over the homework before they leave because it was a kick ass assignment on scansion and God knows they need more practice with that and Mallory is so freaking brilliant I must remember to follow her career because that girl is definitely going to be a writer and maybe she'll even remember that I was the one who got her to read *Lolita* for the first time even if it wasn't in Tehran and the Lacrosse team is being dismissed just prior to the fire drill so I need to tell them to check the website and no, Sam is not on the Lacrosse team because I checked with the coach and he was faking it, and I must try to use the highlighter on the Smartboard because April has to have things in color and her IEP is coming up and her mother is suing the school right now even though no one ever tells me anything I saw a memo someone left by the printer and ole Zach of course needs manipulatives so he can get up and move around, so I have to get him to come up and do the annotation on the board while not losing track of how excellent the line "May one be pardon'd and retain the offense" is and how it really sums up Claudius's dilemma and when Paul asks that precocious question be sure to answer it fully but I can't let him dominate because then the other kids shut down and Jesus God, ole Billy knew how to write and are they getting how fabulous this is? Are they? *Are they?*

12:55: All my classes are pretty much a mad dash through ideas, and by now a giddiness has set in. Half of the things I say in class are now completely inappropriate, because my filters are overloaded. I have literally lost the ability to screen my speech before it slips out. I may even drop the F-bomb if I really get going, as in "You know, Hemingway is so fucking smart, he...." or "Molly, what the fuck kind of an answer is that?"

And guys, if you do drop the F-bomb by accident, and you will, turn it into a teachable moment. I always tell the kids there is a moment for expletives, and you need to be able to identify said moment. For example, I say, when I talk to the principal, I do not drop the F-bomb. No F-ing way (giggles). But when I talk to Tony, my butcher back in Brooklyn, who began every conversation with "Hey, how the fuck are you? You look fucking fantastic. The fuck is going on with you these days?", of course I'm going to let fly. It would be impolite *not* to, since it might make Tony feel as if I thought I were superior, just because I have more education than he does... You see? You're onto linguistics and the subtleties of usage. Teachable moment!

2:10: There is no down time and Jesus God, I have got to pee. So while the kids are working on a poem I decide to break the rules and leave my crap ass trailer classroom to haul ass across the parking lot to the first floor faculty ladies' room for five seconds. As I am hurriedly relieving myself and wondering if the kids are ransacking my desk and if I really did unplug the coffee maker at the house, I see a little piece of paper slide under the door. I can't reach it, so I stab at it with my toe—what the hell is *that*? Turns out it's from Mrs. Schmitt, the assistant librarian. She's waiting outside and *she* really has to go, and could I hurry up?

2:30: I feel as if I have been having a really long, raucous conversation with excellent and convivial friends, the kind of friends who keep me on my toes intellectually. It feels more like play than work, but it takes everything I've got to keep up and get everything done. I sometimes marvel at where this social energy comes from, yet I summon it every morning, because I know that a slow-wittedness from me is death to the class. *I* set the tone. The talk factor is intense. You have got to love the talk.

After the busses leave, I crawl out of my room, walk into the main building and wish desperately that the teachers' room had a mini bar and I could pour myself a scotch. Or that I taught in France, where they actually *can* pour themselves a scotch. Instead I lean in the doorway of Lucy's room and chat for a few minutes about what a goober Jason Javronovich is, but it's really a chance to unwind. If you despise your colleagues, and there is a good chance that you will (see chapter 4), you either have to go straight home and up to your room for the noise to stop, or worse—back to The Bounty. Even if you don't know the waiter at the nice little out of the way coffee shop, he knows *you*. And even when you think you are far enough out of their reach, the kids will find you. One time I was out of town for the weekend with Claire and we were being idiotic in a drugstore, buying scotch, Jujubes and People magazine to take back to the hotel. We were pretty raucous, and I was laughing and saying that it was a good thing my students couldn't see what an f-ing dumbass I was in real life, or they would lose all respect for me, and the cashier says to me, "Actually, I think I was one of your students." Crap. Turns out she was a kid from my Joan Finch days who had dropped out of college to take a menial day job and try to make it as a singer at night. Now I really *felt* like a dumbass.

The tables were turned, however, when I ran into my superintendent at a 7-Eleven while he was buying a carton of Marlboros, a Playboy, and a couple of six packs. He saw me and pretended not to as he hurried out of the store, which is typical superintendent behavior by the way. They never do anything straight up.

The Devil Wore Guidance

Now that I've dispensed with the preliminaries, you're ready to hear about actual classroom teaching. Not to be too gloom and doomy, but there will be days when you will want to shoot the kids, then shoot yourself. You will be reminded of that Stephen King story you once read in which the teacher goes insane from how rotten the kids are and takes each student into a room for a test but then blows the kid's brains out. This story will begin to seem reasonable to you. If you complain that your class is unruly, your principal will take you aside and tell you to "rise above it", which he thinks is him supporting you, but which is really candy-ass for, "I'm afraid of a lawsuit."

Guidance counselors are a queer subset of antagonists. A good one will insist on sitting in the room with you when that parent shows up outside your door without an appointment, because she knows that he's an alcoholic spoiling for a fight. *You* don't know that, so you're all "Sure, let's meet and talk about Samuel's exam," but *she* knows everything that's been going on in the family, and *she* knows that it's going to get bad. When it does get bad, and the parent is shrieking that you are the worst teacher ever, that you don't know your craft, that he only came to school today to check you out and he has found you lacking, this type of guidance counselor will stand up and say, "This meeting is over." She'll walk you out to the parking lot afterward and tell you all the stuff that she's not legally allowed to tell you, but which explains everything and reassures you that you may be young and inexperienced, but you are not the worst teacher in the world. You will still be shaking and sniveling from the encounter, and you'll be shaking and sniveling for a few days after, but thanks to her you will not be destroyed by it. And you'll know that when a parent shows up without an appointment and an angry look on his face, you always ask the guidance counselor or principal to sit in. And keep the door open.

Alas, not all guidance counselors are Tammy Taylor from *Friday Night Lights*. Like mosquitoes, most of them just make your life miserable until you swat them. My friend Kelly Barnes went through her own guidance counselor hell her first year, with a last period of the day class that was out of control:

"So stream of consciousness is Faulkner's technique here..."

"You're a cocksucker!" cries the new kid who just transferred from Florida.

(Giggles. Miss Barnes ignores it) "And if you look at the first paragraph you'll see..."

"Cocksucker!"

(Mad giggles) "...you'll see that the voice is really a thought process with no editing..."

"Fucking c——!"

(Absolute uproar from the kids. Miss Barnes is silent, praying for order.)

"Cock-sucking, mother f——-ing c——!"

Why, you may ask, did Miss Barnes simply not send the kid to the office, or at least the hallway? The kid had Tourettes Syndrome, of course, and according to his parents he was an absolute peach of a kid when he wasn't calling his teacher a cock-sucking c—— in front of the whole class. The problem was that he also had a 504 plan, which allowed him to do whatever the hell he wanted and get away with it. He had a legal right to be in the class, so she'd be teaching along, talking about parallel construction or something, and all of a sudden the kid would shout out some horrible obscenity. So Miss Barnes talked to the kid's guidance counselor, who told her that she wasn't allowed to tell the other kids what was going on, because it's illegal to disclose a student's 504 plan, blah blah blah. Miss Barnes was supposed to just keep teaching, even though the other kids thought there was something wrong with *her*, because she never said anything to the kid.

Finally Miss Barnes had had enough, so she went to the head of guidance to see what could be done about getting around this problem of disclosure. And the head of guidance said there really was no way she could tell the other kids what was going on, but she gave Miss Barnes a strategy (wink wink): Every time the kid said a bad word in class, Miss Barnes was supposed to follow it up immediately with the phrase "B'Gosh, B'Golly". Eventually, the guidance counselor was sure, the kid would be conditioned to adopt this expression in place of his outburst of c-words.

In the end, Miss Barnes decided that she could live with being called a cocksucker in front of the kids, because it sounded better than "B'Gosh B'Golly."

Of course, kids always find out everything you don't want them to know, and so they eventually discovered the new kid's secret. They learned to expect his outbursts, and instead of giggling they'd nod knowingly in agreement. Yes, it was true, the kid had Tourettes, and Miss Barnes really was a cocksucker.

My friend's mistake, of course, was

listening to guidance. What she should have done was hold a sensible, polite meeting with the father in his office, and every few seconds call him a mo-fo, loudly, so all his colleagues could hear it. If he objected, she could explain that she, too, has Tourettes—does it bother him? Is it difficult to concentrate, you son-of-a-bitch? That might have changed his mind about disclosing his kid's illness.

Sigh. This simple, direct approach is not always possible, however.

Sometimes things go wrong and it's your fault. In this case, you need to admit it. If the class is going south it's because you screwed up. Never tell the kids it's their fault because it isn't, and they will, correctly, despise you for saying that it is. You are the person who sets the tone, not them. They are waiting for you to lead them. Anything else makes them uncomfortable. So that sit-in-a-circle and share your life with me crap is not going to cut it. Especially if you didn't take my advice about the haircut, because then they're just passing around hideous drawings of you naked, with a mullet.

No, your only option is to quickly concede that you botched it and change tacks. Here are three foolproof quick fixes when you experience lesson-plan failure and mutiny flares:

1) Quietly get out a red-checked

tablecloth and a baguette and some really good French cheese. Lay the tablecloth out on the floor, sit down and simply begin spreading the cheese on a piece of bread and passing it around. Most kids will be curious enough to try it, and some will even like it. All of them will stop what they're doing to get a look at what *you're* doing. Invite them to join you on the floor for this impromptu picnic. Here comes the kicker—tell them you are evaluating them on their ability to taste this delectable cheese and make polite conversation. Discuss 19th century manners if possible. I have a tiny book on my shelf called *Don't*, which the kids love, because it has rules about removing earwax, extricating food from your moustache, and how to avoid shocking the ladies (don't use your champagne glass as a spittoon, guys). When things have settled, inform them that knowing how to eat and converse is the secret to having a good life. Ask them what they think Mr. Keller's chemistry class is doing right now, then ask them if this isn't better. If you don't have any French cheese lying around ripening, you can substitute red caviar and good unsalted butter. You've got them now, you are setting the tone, they are comfortable with it, and from there you can go anywhere. This also works very well with an individual troublemaker. (Dustin, if you are reading this, remember the time I invited you to have lunch with me? You thought it was a detention but then when you showed up I had roast chicken and baked potatoes and carrots, a tablecloth and real napkins. We ate lunch, we talked about your motorcycle and you never gave me a hard time in class again.)

2) Throw down whatever book is not working and look them in the eye and say, "Screw this. Let's just talk." (Actually, sometimes if you can tell a class is going to give you a hard time, start reading a book that you *know* they'll hate, then after a half an hour chuck it across the room and pronounce it to be pretentious crap. They will be putty in your hands for the rest of the year.) Then get out a piece of paper and put all their names on it in a list. Tell them that you are going to throw out a topic, and they are going to take turns speaking on the topic. If they speak three times, they get an A. If they speak twice, they get a B. Once is a C, no speaking at all is a D, and any form of interruption or distraction is an F. They will be incredulous—"Is that all we have to do to get an A?"—but before you know it you are having a brilliant discussion and everyone is participating. (Ok, maybe it's not brilliant, but for some kids, any discussion at all is brilliant.) All you have to do is put a little check mark next to the kid's name every time he says

something. And listen, really listen, because they will say stuff that you could not make up if you tried, and you might want to put it in a book someday. Like when we were talking about why people bother to read fiction and Tyler Bedigian said, "To get to the end."

3. This is only for really high energy types, and you need a good sound system. When you've lost control of the class and it's starting to get loud, you have to be louder, but shouting just makes you look stupid. Instead, put on a really rockin' song and crank it up, then grab the girls and make them line up. Line up the boys, and teach them how to dance. Personally, I prefer swing, but you could teach them the funky chicken if you like. They will resist, but when you select one kid from the crowd to be your partner, you will get their attention and they will be so grateful that you didn't pick them for your guinea pig, they will gladly cooperate. After ten minutes of instruction, have a contest. Yaya's are out, everyone's in a good mood, and you've taught them a valuable social skill. It works every time. N.B.: Do not substitute your own folksy, maudlin guitar strummin' for the real thing. No one wants to hear you wail "They Paved Paradise" or "Puff The Magic Effing Dragon".

Do not expect the kids to change anything they are doing, because they won't. If they're talking on their cell phones, they will continue to do so until it no longer benefits them. If they're yakking about Saturday night's party out at the rifle range, they'll keep on doing that until it's no longer the most interesting thing to talk about. If they are putting their heads down on the desk and snoring, they'll keep that up until it's no longer viable. Your job is to make sure that it never is viable.

When things are *really* goin' south, like way past Mexico and straight to hell, you need to pull out your secret strength. You may recall that idiotic film, *Dangerous Minds,* in which Michelle Pfeiffer loses the class and so she writes on the board "I know karate." Well, that was her character's secret strength. Secret strength is the weird quirk you have that no one knows about because you keep it secret until you reach crisis point, like in chess. (I don't know exactly how it is like chess, but just go with it.)

I got through my first year of teaching with the help of two fabulous, altruistic colleagues and a lot of luck. There was one afternoon, however, when my colleagues weren't around and my luck had run out for a drink with fortune, so I was alone when Dylan VanBrundt came to the door. He was dumb as a post and quite jacked for a seventeen-year-old. All he had goin' for him was washboard abs and huge hands, and he knew it. It was the spring of his senior year, and he had been rejected from every school to which he'd applied, probably because of his open aspiration to become a professional assassin. He wanted to get a copy of the resume I'd had all my seniors create, in case they needed a summer job. In class he'd ignored me and done the bare minimum on the assignment, thinking he'd be accepted to the US Special Forces or MI-5 or something. After asking the students to copy and save it on their thumb drives, I had deleted his resume along with all the others. Dylan chucked *his* thumb drive out the window. He had flunked my class due to fear and arrogance, and now it was three o'clock, we were all alone, the room was hot, he was furious at the world and at me for being in it, and we both knew it.

"What do you mean you deleted it?" he demanded.

"I'm sorry, but I don't have it any more. I asked you to save it, and you didn't want to."

(Long stare) "Get it back."

(Nervous, involuntary chuckle) "Dylan, I can't. I can help you write it again, but there is no way to just get it back. It's gone."

It was then that I noticed his right hand clenching into a fist. I could see the long cord of muscle in his bare arm grow taut. I started to

100

move through the doorway, thinking he would back out and let me by, but instead he stretched his arm across to block me. He began to mutter something to himself, in that creepy way he had when he was getting frustrated.

And it was at that moment that I recalled the charming fable of Tina and Mrs. Finch, and my secret strength came to me: Brooklyn. Every basic instinct was on code red, and I went into a mode that I had once used with a mugger on Flatbush Avenue.

"Get the hell out of my way. *Now*," I said.

I waited for the first blow, wondering what it would actually feel like to have a hard fist slam into my face. Instead, he backed out of the doorway and walked off, muttering and slamming lockers as he went.

I shook all the way home, but I can tell you this. Old Joanie baby Finch was right. Sometimes you have to channel your secret strength, so be ready. Sometimes you have to forget you're a teacher and just be a person. You gotta act on instinct. *Instinct*, kiddo. It could save your ass.

Let's Misbehave

When I first started teaching I was, like you, an idiot.

I worried all the time about what I was going to be doing next, if parents were going to find out that I was a big fat fake, and whether or not the kids liked me. (Now everyone *knows* I'm a huge fat fake, and kids? What are "kids"?) I would go to dinner with friends Saturday night and while they chatted on about their jobs and their lives, I was rehashing Friday, period 8, when I had overheard Elijah Butnick telling another kid that I was a "douche on wheels." (Typical kid--his insulting metaphors are mixed, cliché, and lacking precision.) I knew I should let it go, but instead I actually worried about Elijah Butnick, because his parents were on to me. They'd already complained about me to the principal. Their complaint was unusual, they admitted, but they insisted that it be addressed nonetheless. You see, Elijah was deeply disturbed not by my brutal vocabulary quizzes or my relentless insistence on revising, nor was he troubled by the subtleties of the Emerson essay I was making him annotate. Mom and Dad were not even concerned wth the possibility that I may in fact have actually *been* a douche on wheels.

They actually complained because Elijah did not like the smell of my deodorant. I kid you not—they said that little Elijah couldn't do his work because he was offended by *Sure: Regular Scent.*

I'm telling you, parents will say anything to avoid admitting that their child is a turd. Have you ever heard of a parent saying, "I'm sorry my son has been such a shit. We have done a horrible job with him and now he's pretty much ruined, but you shouldn't have to put up with him. Here's a nice bottle of Zin to ease your pain."

I thought not.

So I worried about Elijah Butnick, and his parents, and how I was going to face him with dignity on Monday (*Secret for Women? Old Spice? Irish Freaking Spring?*), when I should have been spending the weekend doing what YOU should be doing on your weekends: misbehaving.

The reasoning here is pretty basic: all week long you are a paragon of propriety, a flipping school marm. And people have not changed their notions of what a teacher is like since 1620, by the way. Most people still think teachers are really "good people" who "love kids" and "want to help others." You are supposed to stand for the pledge, discourage promiscuity, insist that smoking is awful and demonize alcohol like the rest of America. You're supposed to respect diversity, make good choices, and dress respectably, so the boys don't stare at your cleavage. Most jobs don't ask you to be a saint, but this one does.

And not only do you have to pretend to buy into all this Mother Theresa garbage all week, your superintendent is going to ask that you not go downtown on your personal day, because *people might see you.*

That's right--people might actually see you. Teachers, apparently, are supposed to remain invisible. People might see you sitting in a coffee shop or buying Johnny B at the liquor store, or trying on bras at Victoria's Secret. Then the news would be all over town: you don't really care about other people's children very much, and you do in fact have a life outside of school that sometimes requires a decent bra, and you actually use your personal days, to which you are legally entitled. Your superintendent will tell you that no one wants to see a teacher not working.

The public does not want a teacher to be a person.

It's perfectly all right, however, if you decide to spend your Saturday night at the school concert, or chaperoning a dance. You're supposed to want to do that to support other people's kids.

Repeat: What are "kids"?

So I would now like to put in a word for drinking, swearing, smoking, and generally doing everything you're not allowed to do or even supposed to *want* to do as a role model for young adults. But the truth is, you are going to be a better teacher if you occasionally let fly.

By November of my first year on the job, I was ready to stop being a martyr. I'd been spending hours trying to figure out my learning objectives (complete waste of time), and of course, reading the three different novels and trying to figure out what was worth teaching in each one. Then on Friday morning it came-- the absolutely delicious ring-a-ding ding at 5:30. The 5:30 call is always good (as compared to the 2:30 am call, which never is), because it always means Snow Day.

A snow day is the one perk that teachers get to be smug about. All those corporate drones have to drag it in no matter what, but teachers at least once a year, if they live in the Northeast anyway, get paid to stay home and do nothing.

And all because teenagers can't drive in the snow.

So I got the call, and of course afterward I decided to loll in bed for a while, then I got up, read the paper, had a cup of coffee, watched all of Season 5 of *Game of Thrones*. There was a stack of essays to be graded lying in my pitiful teacher briefcase, and I just could not face them. So instead I rearranged my living room (Ikea couch in the corner, Ikea couch against the wall, Ikea couch in the middle of the room), got rid of all my cruddy t-shirts and, spinster that I was, washed my kitchen floor, then took a shower. Then I stood around watching the snow fall outside and being bored. It was indeed a blizzard out there, so there was no way I was going to cruise TJ's or Old Navy. Instead, I thought I would take out the trash.

I was so focused on the white out and how I would Wuthering Heights it to the garage to put the trash in the bin, that I did not notice when the door clicked behind me. A few moments later I was standing on my back porch in my bathrobe, snow boots and nothing else, jiggling the doorknob.

Not good.

As my damp hair stiffened in the 20-degree blast, I realized that it sucked to be new to, well, anywhere, but especially to be a half-naked school teacher in a tiny town in a blizzard. Christ, where was Claire when I needed her? Probably at Balthazar having a grapefruit cosmo and the blini with fig compote.

I knew I had to get inside before my hair froze to a mailbox or something, so I tromped across the still unplowed street and rang the door of the other crappy ranch house in the hood. The people next door to my own crappy ranch house had two rotten kids, and I definitely did not want to see other people's kids on my day off.

A plump young woman answered the door, took one look at the bathrobe and boots get up, and snorted.

"What are *you* selling?" she asked. I introduced myself and explained who I was, and how I was locked out. Candace, my new best friend as of the two minutes I spent on her porch, was a navy wife and was happy to let me in. She had, literally, been around the world a few times and was not flabbergasted by much. I explained that I had no way of re-entering my house, and we agreed that after a cup of coffee and the use of her blow dryer we'd trudge back to my house and Candace would use her credit card to break in.

We did, it worked, and in return for her hospitality, I asked her to have another cup of coffee with me. I had nothing else to do, and neither did she, so pretty soon we were yakking like two crows on a branch. I liked her—she was spunky and she had a really great laugh. We covered a lot of ground and quickly moved on to how men are pigs and how her mother-in-law was a cow. Then she pulled a joint out of her pocket and asked me if I wanted to party.

You may not believe this, but I actually do not imbibe, as a rule. No moral here, just not that interested. Once, in college, but I laughed for five minutes hysterically then fell asleep, so I had stayed away from pot ever since. Truth be told, I wasn't really sure if I was *capable* of getting high.

It was Candace The Navy Wife Across the Street who encouraged me to temporarily shed my fear of the law and my goody-two-shoes role as public servant and embrace my inner Dead Head. The snow was still falling heavily and there were no cars on our little street, and even the rotten kids next door were probably holed up with *Frozen* or something. The whole town seemed lost in a snow globe world and so Candace and I toked up, and then it started.

It turns out Candace's husband was a pothead himself, and often brought back samples of narcotics and hallucinogens from around the globe. This particular batch was from the Melkweg, a nighclub in Amsterdam where apparently you can get just about anything. After two puffs it was clear that this was not your average American Maryjane. I tried to get up and get another cup of coffee, but by the time I got to the counter I could not remember if I'd already drunk it. Candace, like a pudgy version of a Manet, was stretched out on my Ikea couch. This now seemed hilarious because the couch was in the middle of the room, and we were both laughing. My stomach was starting to ache from laughing so hard, and it occurred to me that laughter was actually a good form of exercise. I was convinced that if we kept this up, I would have a perfect bikini bod by spring.

And *that* made me think of this stupid workout tape that Claire had given me a while back, called "Do It to The Music, Featuring KC and The Sunshine Band," which I decided Candace and I needed to enjoy. A moment later we had ransacked the bag of old t-shirts that was supposed to go to the Salvation Army and then there we were: jumping around the Ikea couch in our underwear and cruddy t-shirts, to the thumping refrain of "That's the Way, Uh-huh. Uh-huh, I Like It."

"Push it!" Candace shrieked, as she squatted then popped up like a stoned jack in the box. My cheap floors groaned under her enthusiastic leaps.

"That's the way, uh-huh, uh-huh, I like it!" I sang, twirling around. I somehow had acquired a plastic martini glass, and I still had the joint in my other hand. I didn't know it at the time, but I was letting off some serious new teacher steam. God, it felt great to be bad!

Suddenly my doorbell rang. Candace stopped jumping and put her hand to her mouth to stop from laughing. "Shhhh!" she hissed. Then her eyes got very large and she dashed behind the kitchen counter and crouched down.

"What the f..." I started to say, then the doorbell rang again. I looked at Candace, who had generated a puddle of pee and slid down into it. She was still laughing, the kind of laugh that, indeed, creates great abs.

"Who is it...?" I sang out as I sailed down the hall to the door, still flushed and giddy from the exhilarating vocal stylings of KC. I thought it would be hilarious to take a deep puff then open the door and blow it in the face of whoever had dared to intrude on our exercise session. I swung the door open, posed Deitrich-style, and blew out as much smoke as I could. As I felt the rush of cold air on my bare legs I realized that I was looking at a middle-aged couple in overcoats, all frosted with snow.

"Are you Ms. Danner?" the woman asked, confused.

"Darling, I am," I said stupidly. Already my jubilee was wearing off, but then I remembered Candace sitting in her own urine on my new kitchen floor and I started giggling again.

"We're Martin's parents," the woman said tersely. "He was sick yesterday, and he asked us to drop off his essay. He said that you said it was ok to bring it to your house. We live just down the street."

In fact, what I had said, while on my high, new-teacher-drunk-with-power horse, was that I didn't care *how* sick a kid was, that even if the kid was dead, I would dig him up, and make him turn in that essay, so if they were planning on faking sick and not showing up in class because they hadn't done the work they had better bring it right to my door.... and indeed Martin had done just that. Kids are so freaking literal.

Martin's father never said a word, but just stared bug-eyed at the martini glass and the joint.

"Oh." I said.

Long pause.

Martin's mom handed me a plastic bag with a manila folder in it. "Thanks," I said.

Push it! Push it good! blasted from the living room.

"Have a nice evening," Martin's mom said, and they left.

It was funny for another twenty minutes, then it wasn't, then the whole thing was just plain disturbing. I kicked Candace out and cleaned my kitchen floor for the second time that day. I think I went to bed at about 7:30 that night, after I ate an entire box of Rice Crispies. Or thought I did.

The next week was some of my best teaching of that year. I was focused, I was organized, I was razor sharp. I was also scared senseless that I would be fired. Still, something inside me that needed to go off had indeed exploded, and now I was easier with my role as a role model.

I'm just sayin': sometimes you got to be bad to be good.

Never Underestimate the Weird Kid

As a public-school teacher, you are going to see some freaky stuff. Every teacher remembers the first really bizarre kid. And you must never underestimate the weird kid.

Earl Becker, by far my weirdest kid ever, happened to me my first-year teaching. Earl was born, the product of incest, in the back of a truck. His parents didn't see much hope in his prospects, so they left him at a Salvation Army booth in the parking lot of a mall and kept on driving. The nearest hospital was two hundred miles away, so the attendant brought Earl to his church, and that same afternoon he was taken in, unofficially, by Mrs. Eugene Becker, a church member in good standing. Earl was twenty-four hours old; Mrs. Becker was seventy-five.

Through some complex but loosely woven tapestry of state regulations, and due to the fact that Earl was an albino and had a rare blood disease that promised a life span comparable to that of a large dog, Mrs. Becker was allowed to raise Earl as her ward. She was a widow, and her husband had left her with a modest pension from the paper mill. She lived in a rundown three-bedroom ranch on the edge of town in a neighborhood that remained undeveloped. She kept budgies, a gramophone, and window boxes of pansies. Driving past the Becker house you had the unnerving sensation that it was 1932.

"I see you've got Earl in Creative Writing," the librarian said at the coffee and doughnut thing before the first day of classes. She was smiling cryptically through large, rimless glasses and I suspected I had inherited some hellion, or perhaps a senator's son. I couldn't tell.

"Is there something I need to know about this kid?" I asked.

"You've got to see for yourself," she said with a wink. "He's unique."

In my experience, things labeled "unique" rarely turn out to be the only one of their kind, unparalleled, or impossible to duplicate. Nonetheless, it was a word I would hear several times before the day was through, and always in connection to Earl Becker. It was the only adjective anyone could drum up to describe him.

I spotted him immediately the next morning. His appearance was astonishing. If Snow White had had a pygmy brother, Earl Becker was it. He lurched toward me, hugging the wall and muttering to himself. He wore a dark jacket and pleated pants, a blue bow tie, and—I kid you not—wingtips. He even smelled like

1932—a milk bottle, wool suit smell. His skin, the color of creme fraiche, had the moist, glistening pallor usually found on the underbelly of a frog. The head had been plopped onto the shoulders without the bother of a neck, and as a result, he stooped like a hunchback. At the forehead there was a violent shift from pasty pale skin to jet black, glossy hair that sat on his skull like molded plastic: a permanent pompadour. He had ghastly red lips and a tendency to spit when he talked.

"Mith Danner, I prethume," he croaked as he reached out to shake my hand. His skin was clammy. He looked at me slyly, sizing me up to see if I were friend or foe, and took a front row seat in the class. The seats on both sides of him remained empty.

After my initial bumbling introduction, my expectations, a breakdown of my grading system, and a muddling diagnostic writing assignment, Earl raised his hand.

"Do you know Freddie Mercury, Mith Danner?"

"Of course. Lead singer of Queen." This was good—I could talk rock and roll history if my inane lesson on punctuating dialog failed.

"He was from Zanzibar," Earl stated, beaming. His mouth was a horrible little cave lined with mossy stones. While I contemplated its depths I waited for some relevance to the topic at hand—the proper use of single quotes—but none followed. Apparently the exotic locale of Freddie's birth was the salient point.

I soon discovered there was a theme. While students were in the library researching historical settings for their stories, I noticed that one of the encyclopedia Britannica was missing. Sure enough, there was Earl Becker, scrunching himself up very small in a chair at the back of the room, his eyes circumspectly peering over the rim of volume eleven, the letter "Z". When I approached him he pressed his plump, gibbous body into the upholstery with the success of a cat hiding behind a penny.

"Did you know, Mith Danner, that Freddie Mercury was Persian?" His moony face tilted up at me with sheer wonder. "Perrrrsian," he repeated dreamily.

"That's interesting. Why do you like Freddie Mercury so much?" I asked.

To my surprise, he became agitated when directly confronted, and he abruptly got up and walked off.

I cannot claim any intellectual or social success with Earl Becker. In class he remained elusive, as immutable as stone. Despite sensitive after-class conversations in which I attempted to draw him out, more structured assignments designed to lead him toward the course content and even explicit threats ("You are going to flunk this elective, Earl, you really, really, *really* are, I am not kidding..."), he stuck to his theme, and he did not interact with other kids. I also noticed that he signed his name Blaze Gorton on his written work. This turned out to be the name of a shadowy comic book artist.

Despite his narrowness of topic, Earl showed an impressive range in conversational openers, which he sprung on me before class, or in the cafeteria, where he always sat alone.

"Did you know, Mith Danner, that there are thtartling parallels between the Kennedy and Lincoln athathinathions?"

"Did you know, Mith Danner, that Coppertone was invented by a bald doctor who tried it out on hith own head?"

"Did you know, Mith Danner, that amphibianth lack thcales?"

I could only imagine the kind of life that would be so obsessed with obscurity. After walking home from school alone, he would probably have a snack at the enamel kitchen table while his doting ninety-year-old guardian looked on. Then he would toddle to his room and immerse himself in his 45s (that's a small vinyl record, young one) until supper, which was usually fabricated out of a can of cream of mushroom soup. In the evenings, I felt certain, the two misfits must have listened to the radio or played dominoes. Mrs. Eugene Becker would retire early, leaving Earl alone with his thoughts for hours. Did he write novels in his lair? Did he invent motorized mousetraps in the basement? Perhaps he fantasized about a girl. Maybe he stared at the moon and strummed the ukulele. I could never bear to contemplate his miserable existence for long. Like all first-year teachers, I was wildly inefficient, so I didn't have time.

Then one day I saw something that made me realize just how miserable he was. He was languishing in the hallway just after lunch. He always lingered against a wall, a shade in the world of the living, and I almost turned away but then he did something so extraordinary I couldn't stop staring. A girl in a red sweater was reaching into her locker for something and Earl scuttled behind her, crablike, then reached out and touched her hair. As she turned on him he recoiled and raised his arms up to his face in an attitude of Quasimodo.

"Don't touch me, freak!" she yelled.

There were no gargoyles or apostles to look down on the scene, but it was gothic all the same. The girl stormed past him and he watched her walk away. His ghastly face wore the overturned crescent of tragedy, and his lips curled into an apelike leer. I stepped into my classroom and shut the door, half expecting him to climb onto the school roof to rage at passing planes.

I got used to Earl after that. Rather than a daily riddle to solve, he was just a familiar presence in the building, like a poltergeist long accepted as harmless by the inhabitants of the castle. Aside from the one time I saw some older boys shoving him into the mouth of a tuba, I gave him a B and didn't intervene in his life. I left that to others with more training in academic exotica.

The high school talent show, a gym crammed with antsy teenagers at the end of the long week before Thanksgiving, is something for which graduate school cannot prepare you. There is a weird sensation of deja vu as you find yourself leaning up against the back wall, no longer a participant. You feel that tug of adulthood, the odd awareness of teacherhood, and at the same time the powerful remembrance of what it was like to be among the glandularly challenged. I stood there awkwardly, not yet familiar enough with the students to adopt the relaxed posture of authority that later would come naturally. I was still new to this world, and I remember being shocked that high school had carried on after I had finished with it. Kids still ripped around gymnasiums, skidding on sneakers, grabbing at their friends or clustering like mice in dark corners. They still shrieked and lunged, or stood there twitching, ready to combust.

Finally the lights in the gym went out and the chaos subsided into a dull background rumble of shifting chairs and whisperings. The curtains came up and there was the stage—bare and unforgiving, as only a high school stage can be. Two girls in peasant dresses came on first, one sang and the other played a lifeless, forgettable ballad on the guitar. Then there was a group of five rattling out a self-conscious version of "Take the A Train" on their wind instruments. A girl dance combo, another soloist, a magic act, a few technical difficulties which resulted in the band teacher clomping on stage to plead for patience and cooperation, then a long stretch of nothing but harsh lights and a dead microphone snaked across the stage.

In the midst of audience restlessness, Earl stepped out from behind the curtain fringe wearing his wingtips and undertaker's suit, puffed to the middle of the stage and picked up the snake. I looked around nervously. Was he supposed to be doing that? No one seemed to notice. Please, *please* don't start in on Freddie Mercury, I prayed.

An earsplitting peal rent the room as Earl brought the microphone up to his moist, froggy lips.

What happened next can only be explained by the curious paradox of adolescence, which states that those who lack social appeal are compelled by the force of hormones to exhibit their deficiency amplified, in front of hundreds. I was suddenly possessed by an urge to storm up on stage and shield this creature from a cruel crucifixion-death by sarcasm—for Earl Becker was in violation of "cool."

I was prevented from doing so by a terrifying sound.

"How you feelin' tonight, Vegath?" he croaked, thpitting on the mike.

The crowd ignited into one solid scream.

I gasped as Earl suddenly lunged onto his knees and raised one arm high in the air in a bizarre salute to the ceiling. The kids watched, Earlerized. Any second now, I thought, someone would shout something, probably a tough senior boy, and it would all fizzle into your basic humiliation fest.

It didn't.

Instead, that pasty face contorted into hideous grimace, the double chin tilted upward as he looked to the ceiling for a sign. There was another metallic microphone screech, then a wickedly loud, primal drumbeat started and Earl Becker leapt to his feet and pounded downstage like a possessed troll, lip-synching the words to Peter Gabriel's "Sledgehammer". He strutted, he swaggered, at one point he turned his back to the audience and shook his behind while girls screamed in delight. Overcome with passion during an instrumental riff, he chucked the microphone to the floor, twisted out of his suit jacket, gave it a good wind up, and hurled it into the audience. Kids leapt to grab the jacket, and one boy finally wrestled it out of the air from another. The kids were watching the commotion, but I could not take my eyes off Earl Becker, crawling across the stage like a special ed version of Wyeth's *Christina's World*, his pale, flabby face positively smirking.

Did he *know* they were mocking him?

Were they mocking him?

Or was he some sort of mad mascot, the high school's own anti-hero? The faces around me were upturned and happy; the kids were giddy and swept away by the force of Earl's exuberance. A group of boys climbed onstage and lifted him onto their shoulders. After a moment of uncertain equilibrium, he lay his head back in ecstasy, his arms spread limp and Christ-like at his sides, his obscene white stomach protruding from an opening in his polyester shirt.

Perhaps in a talent show on a pre-vacation Wednesday afternoon they would allow it, this bizarre aberration of the social order. Maybe they saw something in Earl that I didn't—some unfulfilled promise, a positive energy that would shoot out into the world and explode into acceptable or at least tolerable form some day. Or maybe there is some mass empathy that can happen, like mass hysteria, when people gather around a compelling backbeat. The pounding catharsis of a Peter Gabriel song could be the secret to ending the war in the Middle East, if only we could harness it!

I finally decided that there was no explanation for the sudden rise of Earl Becker. I felt oppressed by the heat and noise and intensity of my profession. I moved toward the exit, weakened and humbled by what I had seen, knowing that I knew nothing, hoping I would figure it out by Monday.

The Horrible Thing They Will Ask You to Do

At some point you might have to do the most horrible thing a teacher has to do: serve on a committee. Everyone knows that this is a colossal waste of time and resources, so of course everyone plunges ahead unquestioningly. There are all sorts of committees, and superintendents LOVE it when you join one, because that means you are INVOLVED (Good job!). Here is the trick: Go ahead and sign up for them, then just don't go to the meetings.

It sounds risky, like you'll get caught, but you won't, I'm telling you. I've been on tons of committees, and I go to the first session, then I bail. Teachers won't say anything because they get it. Committee heads don't want to acknowledge that their committee is actually so pointless that people don't even show up, so *they* won't say anything. Also, your absence means they have more power, which is why they volunteered to be the committee head in the first place, so they are actually psyched that your mouthy little face is not there. If you're lucky, the whole thing just dissolves. I served on a committee for several years that never met. It can happen.

If, however, your school is up for accreditation, you are screwed. Accreditation is when an outside entity comes to check on you and make sure the school is up to snuff. When this happens the school starts sweating bullets, and the bad teachers start worrying because it means that teachers from other schools will come into their classrooms and find out what rotten teachers they are. It won't happen immediately, because accreditation is a serious, long-winded affair that involves the whole school and People from The State and the National Accreditation Grand Poobah. Everyone must participate, you are told, so later they can say that you actually had a voice in the affair, which of course, you don't. You will be informed of this impending time-guzzler at a faculty meeting. It goes like this:

Our principal, Mr. Laverdiere, holds us hostage after school one day and tells us that it is our year to be scrutinized. We must work together on passing accreditation. Jennifer, a spunky biology teacher with a swingy pageboy haircut, raises her hand and asks how much money this will cost the town. She doesn't say it like that, but we all know what she means. Laverdiere does not like this question—no administrator does. It's like asking a presidential candidate for his position on abortion. So he stares at her for a moment, wishing he had hired the dumber candidate. We look at Jennifer, and we look at Laverdiere, which is like watching Jackie Chan trying to decide whether or not to bluff in Texas Hold 'Em.

"I believe the total is something like thirty-five thousand," he says, cornered.

We gasp.

"But that's one full-time, first-year teacher's salary," says the social studies aide, who is sitting in front of me. She is impressed with the injustice of it. She is just low enough on the totem pole to still look up to full-time teachers. We higher-order thinkers, however, are merely horrified that you can actually get someone to work for so little. (Remember, don't ever say your real salary out loud, and never, *never* look at your pay stubs, or you will quit on the spot. I just shove mine into a drawer.)

There is a general twittering in the crowd, until Laverdiere tells us that he knows it's a colossal waste of precious resources because we know we're a decent school, our test scores prove it, plenty of our kids go to Harvard and Yale and all, and even though he does in fact have the power to veto the accreditation, and although the school board would probably be sympathetic since this is a budget crisis year (it always is), he has decided in one spineless swoop that we will go through with it anyway. This kind of warped decision-making logic is in fact taught at leadership seminars, you realize. I once walked in on one by mistake and I actually *saw* them teaching it! I was too embarrassed to sneak out of the room so I sat there and watched the principals drink the Kool-Aid.

Two weeks later the thing I fear the most happens at last. I have been found out, dragged from my trailer, hauled from the hay and plonked onto the table with an apple in my mouth. The Powers That Be have realized that I actually have no interest in pedagogy (does anyone?), that the only thing I am really interested in is reading and writing about great books with students, so they have decided that I must adjust my attitude. I learn this as I am standing outside the door of Laverdiere's office, waiting to use the administrative copy machine because all the other ones are broken again, and I swear to God this is what I hear.

Pete, my department head: Put Danner on a committee. She never does anything.

Laverdiere, incredulous: She doesn't? C'mon, she must do *something*.

Pete: No, I have her file right here and she hasn't done a goddamned thing since we hired her. Looks like she hasn't done anything in her personal life, either. She's a drone, all she does is teach English, and make dinner once a week.

Laverdiere: Just once? Who cooks the rest of the time?

Pete: Her cat.

Laverdiere: You got any other dirt on her?

Pete: Yeah. Turns out she didn't play high school sports, and she was kicked out of Girl Scouts *and* Brownies. (Sadly, this is true. Freaking fascist organizations.)

Laverdiere: Ok. Let's make her a co-chair on that committee with Sully. He never does anything either.

I, the new girl, am now a co-chair. The actual name of the committee is long, some sort of acronym, and I am co-chairing it with Tim Sullivan, the silver fox, whose reputation for sophomoric high jinx has preceded him. He is one of the old boys, and thus can get away with having a little 'tude. We are supposed to be examining the school's new mission statement, discoursing meaningfully with people from other disciplines, and fostering collegiality (it's all in the verbs, apparently). Since we are idiots, this has all been broken down for us into thirteen discussion tasks. According to Kendra, an ebullient middle-aged frump who is head of the steering committee, these tasks will take us three workshop days to complete. *Three days of drinking the Kool-Aid.*

In our first meeting, I make popcorn and sulk, listening to Kendra grind away on the usefulness of this pointless pursuit. Kendra wants us to get behind the thing, to really "effect change." She is fluent in edu-speak, and she alone has a handle on the political maneuvering that the job requires. She has been an Educational Consultant, which makes her better than the rest of us. She's got hair that doesn't move when she shakes her head and she dresses like a stewardess, which makes her suspect in my book.

The reason this assignment is pointless is because the mission statement has already been submitted to the school board, and they have already added meaningless palaver to the original meaningless palaver that the faculty submitted and now the thing is plastered all over the walls. It's a done deal. So it occurs to me that I do not believe in the purpose of the committee which I am co-chairing. In fact, I think as I begin to worry a hangnail, this committee is in direct conflict with the other committee I am on—the Academic Standards Committee, which I have never attended but which is nonetheless dedicated to the eradication of meaningless drivel and putting the focus back on content.

As I grapple with this conflict of interest, harboring the slim hope that I might be able to convince Laverdiere to let me out of this committee, the one whose name we don't understand, Kendra is smiling and clutching a tidy little clipboard. This depresses me, so I look down to the mission statement packet on my desk. Then it gets worse.

After brief scrutiny, I conclude that our mission statement is total malarkey. I simply can't buy into it. This is my first really dark moment in teaching, when I realize that if I had only kept my job at the magazine I could be the Editor-in-Chief of *Vogue* by now and Meryl Streep would be playing me in a movie.

The mission statement has several problems. First of all, it's too wordy. It is now, with the school board additions, forty-seven words long. If I had been asked to write the mission statement, I would have come up with two words: Know Stuff. Kids could remember it, and it is a concept that everyone can get behind, as Kendra would say. It would fit on banners. It would glide effortlessly into pop songs that would be hummed in the halls. It could fit nicely into the rhythm of rap, which is essentially monosyllabic in nature, and therefore would reinforce what we have none of but are always so careful to respect: cultural diversity.

Which brings me to the problem of the phrase, "acceptance of diversity," which are three of the forty-seven words. That *sounds* good, but we ain't got none. We're a Wonderbread school. White, white, white. Except for that nice Austrian exchange student we had. On second thought, I decide, maybe this diversity thing will be easy to live up to. I decide I can live with it.

Sentence number three, however, is a humdinger. I cannot buy into the line about how we "value relationships with parents and the community." Even as a new teacher, I know that no teacher wants parental input. I know they told you that you're supposed to have a relationship with the parents and their third cousins once removed and all, but this is hogwash. What teachers want is for parents to teach their kids manners, so when the kids come to school they are ready to form great relationships with *ideas*. Now that would be a valuable relationship to nurture. I don't show up at Johnny's father's office and tell him how to balance the company budget, because I don't know how to do that. And although Johnny's father did attend school a zillion years ago, he has no freaking idea how to teach English to tenth graders, and I want him to keep his cost-efficient ass out of my classroom.

I decide I'd better keep that particular

insight to myself.

The last thing we're supposed to do, Kendra drones, is write a statement about how the school will be better off because of these three days we've squandered on this committee. We've come full circle now and we will generate our own Kool-Aid. I, however, do not think that we will be better off. In fact, I'm certain my students will suffer because I am wasting three precious days on appreciating our non-existent African American students and fostering relationships with parents instead of brushing up my Shakespeare.

"Danner, what do you think we should do first?" It's Sully, my co, looking to me to be the boss. He's the type that always defers to women, but I can't tell if he really thinks he's not as smart as I am or if he's just jerking my chain so he doesn't have to do the work. I decide he's probably as perplexed as I am about the whole concept of discussion tasks (Does that mean we have to talk about it? Talk about *what*? What are we freaking talking about, anyway?), so I say, "let's start by dividing up the tasks so we all know what we're focusing on."

Administrators love the words "task" and "focus", and I am aware that ole Kendra considers herself an administrator, and she is watching me, sizing me up. Not to mention my colleagues, who are looking to me to direct them here, to get them through the next hour. Trouble is, there are thirteen discussion tasks we're supposed to go through and I don't understand the point of any of them. I somehow can't remember what we are discussing. It's hard to rally the troops when you are kind of clueless. And I don't know the troops that well, because, let's face it, I'm a brand new teacher, and how often does *anyone* in my department have time to schmooze with the chemistry teachers? Do chemistry teachers even know how to schmooze?

"There are thirteen tasks, but there are only twelve of us," announces Joe, the new Vice Principal. He replaced Mullens, who, I am still hoping, will take that shot of Stoli with him to the grave. Joe has a head shaped like a lightbulb and used to teach health in a flat-soda sort of way before he went into administration. This numerical discrepancy is genuinely troubling him, but he is pleased that he is first to see this insurmountable obstacle to our success.

"So one person can do two," counters Stephanie. She teaches physics. She's old guard. She likes the straightest path between two points, bing badda boom. You can't push on a rope with her around.

"Let's cross that bridge when we come to

it," I say. "For now, let's just pick which tasks we want and if two people want the same thing they can flip for it."

"I've got a nickel," Clarence says good-naturedly. He's a gym teacher. He sees this as a face-off in hockey. We are all falling into line with our content areas, I realize.

"Hey, look at number ten," says Sully. "This one's for Danner." I stare stupidly at number ten. After sifting through the edu-speak, I figure out that this is for the poor so and so who has to be The Scribe. (They never say writer, for some reason.) The One Who Writes the Report. I realize with horror that Sully's right, this is me.

"I'm not doing it," I say, before I can stop myself. There is an embarrassed silence. Kendra and the others have seen the ugly truth: I am not a team player. I am a self-serving, whiny witch. "English teachers always get stuck doing everything, and we have more work than anyone else," I say. Then I hunch in my chair, waiting for the rotten eggs and mushy tomatoes to fly. I worry that as the new teacher I am not well-liked, and now I am loathed, I think, and it is no longer going to be just Judith Enniger. I'm seen as an outsider, an upstart, an insolent pup (don't worry, I am not going into the dog analogy again). They think I'm an obnoxious, pushy New Yorker and a food snob who eats lunch in her room. Even if there is one person on staff who does not think the new kid is a total prig, this seals it, I decide. I'm a goner.

Miraculously, no one says anything.

"Are you guys just going to *accept* that?" I ask. I am stunned. It's one of the things you're never supposed to do, claim that you work harder than another teacher. We are all supposed to work as hard as the next guy, even though everyone knows that gym teachers do not work at all. Even if they don't believe that an English teacher might possibly work harder than most, they are willing to go along with this, because they know I don't want to be here, that the committee is a pile of dung, that the mission statement is absurd.

"Well, it's true," says Sully, shrugging. "English teachers do work pretty hard." There is a general murmur of affirmation. I look around.

"Pauline? You agree?" Pauline, also old guard, teaches French, and she's a hard-ass.

"Oh yeah," she says. "Absolutely. I taught English for a while, but I hated all that correcting, And all that bad poetry." This gets an appreciative groan from the others.

"Whaddaya say, buddy," Sully prompts Clarence, "How about you? You agree with Danner?"

This is the real test. The gym teacher has

to admit that he does sweet F-all for this to fly.

"No question," he replies cheerily. "Hands down. I mean, I've never corrected anything in my life." Everyone bursts out laughing and Clarence smiles sheepishly, patting his enormous belly.

I am validated at last. Poor, hardworking, new teacher that I am, I have been waiting since September for someone to acknowledge that I work hard. And the Vice Principal heard it! So now he *knows* I work the hardest! I look at Kendra in amazement. Look, I want to say to her, this stupid meeting has accomplished something after all: my peers have been made aware of my superiority to the gym teacher! The gym teacher himself has admitted it! We have broken through some kind of ceiling, maybe not glass, but cheap acoustic tile or something.

Kendra looks as if she has a load in her pants. This sudden swerve toward candor has upset her plans for a report on the mission statement in thirteen discussion tasks, but I am finally starting to feel the collegiality. I am one with my group, baby.

"You guys are fab," I say, meaning it.

"Does that mean you'll write the report?" asks Clarence, grinning. "'Cause you definitely don't want a gym teacher to write it."

"Ok, ok, I'll do it," I say, giddy with

magnanimity. Up till now, I have had no idea how sympathetic my colleagues are. Hell, for friends like these, I'll go the distance. I'll write the bejesus out of that report!

"It's fifteen pages," says Stephanie. Badda bing, badda boom.

"Huh?" I say, still dreamy.

"You'll have to write fifteen pages. They have a model of it right here." She rattles her packet in the air.

"Can they do that?" asks Joe, the Vice Principal. Once again, he is genuinely puzzled.

"Danner can handle fifteen pages," says Sully, smiling at me. Now I *know* he's flattering me because he doesn't want to help me write the damned report. Typical lacrosse coach. Suddenly, I realize that I do not know what Sully teaches. Or if he teaches. He might just be a coach. Can that happen? I want to ask him, but I can't tell him now, in October, that I have no idea what he teaches. I decide to look him up on the school website and find out which department he's in. Maybe he's a rogue cafeteria worker.

"I'm not writing fifteen pages," I say. "That's ridiculous. What can I say for fifteen pages?"

"Just use the phrase 'product indicator' a lot. That oughta take up some space," offers Linda, a sassy art teacher from Texas. She lets out a wicked giggle and we are officially off and running. Suddenly we are all yammering about how idiotic the mission statement is, how lame the task instructions are. Only one person does not enter into the spirit of our meeting, I notice. It is Kendra The Earnest. She is primly watching us caper like magoons around this thing, hee-heeing and scratching our armpits. She is not amused.

"I think it would be helpful if we really examined the language piece to be sure we're all on the same page," she says meekly.

Meek is just her persona, though—she is actually a Bengal tiger who speaks in corporate cliches. I've seen her type before, back in the real world. She'll bring me down, if I'm not careful. I instinctively move closer to Sully, who has suddenly become my best friend.

"If you're confused about the terminology there's a glossary at the back of the packet," she instructs. She doesn't think I'm up to the job of co-chairing, and she's trying to commandeer my meeting. She's actually starting to sit up in her chair, as if she's going to *stand* up. I realize she is still mad because of that comment I made about people named Eunice before I found out it was her mother's name. She stands up and turns to the first page of the glossary expectantly. I hold my breath.

"Oh Christ, we don't need the damned glossary." It's Stephanie. "We know what the words mean, we just think they're stupid." Thank God for Stephanie.

There is a wild eruption from the plebes. I'm back, baby! Screw Kendra!

"Let's just start by choosing which task we want, and if two people want the same thing we'll flip for it," I say, my eyes starting to water with hilarity. I know that no one is going to do this, but I am drunk with power and I like saying it.

"I've still got the nickel," says Clarence, elbow cocked to the flip position.

Kendra smiles tightly and sinks back into her chair, defeated. For the moment.

I clear my throat and try not to guffaw. "Who wants number one: Attach an organizational chart of the school that illustrates how the various components of the school are organized," I read aloud. All twelve heads now bow dutifully over the packets in concentration. I feel a twitching in my head, the little nagging itch I get when I am confronted with imbecilic language. Not wanting to do that smug, English teacher thing, I hold off. But wait—it's too much—I blurt: "Have you ever seen an organizational chart that *didn't* show how the thing is organized?" I explode in snorts, feeling like Dick Van Dyke in the "I Love to Laugh" number from *Mary Poppins.*

"I can draw a map from my room to the bathroom. Is that what they mean by a pathway?" Linda lets rip. The volume in the room soars to baboon-in-heat level.

"What's the point of making a chart that shows how the school is organized? We know how it's organized. This is busy work," Jennifer the biology teacher calls out from her spot in the corner, where she has been quietly correcting papers. I make a mental note of how impressed I am that she has been following this conversation at all. She's also right, of course. I should really get to know Jennifer, I think. She seems smart. And such a rebel. Why haven't I invited her over to dinner? She might be my new best friend, not that anyone could replace Claire, of course. I wonder if she'd like my house. She teaches biology, but we can still be friends. After all, a lot of doctors became writers: Chekhov, Bertrand Roueche, my friend Jeff from college...

"Oh. My. God," says Stephanie. Her hand slowly rises in a gesture of disbelief and revulsion. "Read number eight you guys. Oh. My. God."

The room quiets down as we rush to get to discussion task number eight. We cannot turn the pages fast enough. We are caught up in a frenzy of the absurd.

"Students must be able to recite the mission statement of the school," she reads. We are dumbstruck. The mission statement? The forty-seven syllables of crappy writing and meaningless drivel? *Recite it?*

"But it's a whole paragraph," says Joe, who seems to have forgotten that he is there to make sure that we take the work seriously, since the administration, rightly, does not trust us.

"And it's stupid," Stephanie adds. This is too much—it's simply too funny. We're off and running again, whooping it up. Linda's round face is turning cherry red and she is twinkling with merriment because Clarence is now imitating a student with severe emotional problems reciting the mission statement to the principal. The room has evolved into "Officer Krupke" from West Side Story. I am on the verge of getting up to tap dance when someone says, "Excuse me, but don't you think we'd better get through this?"

It's Killjoy Kendra. She is still there.

"Ok. Kendra's right. Let's just pick the tasks and call it a day," I say. It's just about time to go home anyway. My first ever meeting as a co-chair is over. The other half of the chair is reading Popular Mechanics, which of course strikes me as funny, but I don't laugh. I don't dare look at Linda or I know I will crack up.

Instead, I keep my eyes straight ahead and say, deadpan, "If two people want the same task, we'll flip for it."

"I've got that nickel right here," says Clarence, right on cue.

Of course, nothing was accomplished and everyone left with a sense of futility, which is fairly typical, I now know. When you're a new teacher, you're too afraid to admit that half the stuff you must do as a faculty is a complete waste of time. You have to remember that you are working for The State, people, and The State is one messed up organization. Bizarre academic mandates come out of meetings where no one in the room is or ever has been a classroom teacher. Forms must be filled out so they can be unfilled out the next week, then edited and filled out again. Simple terms like "research" are defined, and then redefined, and then those definitions are voted on. Later the definition will go into the report on which you will sign your name. This kind of crap takes hours, and *no one ever knows what they do with the reports.* So it goes. Don't let it get you down. After all, in my case, I bonded with my colleagues for the first time, I chatted with people from other disciplines, and we did, technically, discuss the mission statement, which I *think* was the original purpose for the meeting. Most of all, though, the whole rigmarole reminded me that even good students will behave badly when the task itself lacks integrity.

If You Accidentally Commit a Felony...

Sometimes you have to stop teaching the kids
so you can figure out how to teach them. It
usually happens around Christmas time. You're
strung out, you've been full speed ahead for four
months now, and you've hit a dry patch. You're
bored with the next novel on the curriculum, the
kids are bored with you, and they start begging
you for a field trip. So this is a win win. You get a
day when you can actually have lunch in a
restaurant, and they get to take a road trip,
which they love.

The *very* first field trip I ever took was with
my Joan Finch sophomores, when I was a
student teacher. They wanted to eat at an Indian
restaurant after reading Siddhartha (which, like
most heavy-handed allegories, is a complete
snore. See? I developed my own take on it!)
Long story short: I arrive early, get the big table,
wait a humiliatingly long time, then eat chicken
tikka by my lonesome, because not one kid
showed. Was it the novel's fault, my fault, or just
the way kids are? Maybe it was just the way
those kids were. I didn't care—I decided to never
be a sucker again, teach Siddhartha again, or
order chicken tikka at that place again.

By October of my first year of real teaching, I was ready to try it again. I'd heard the legend, of course, of how five years earlier the science field trip had crashed and burned when a boy ate a peanut and went into anaphylactic shock and died on the bus, right in the teacher's arms. I'd also read in the paper how that kid sleepwalked off the balcony in Paris and died. Then there was that girl who got mugged at gunpoint on a school trip to Brazil and didn't die, but she ended up in a mental hospital. Then there were the lesser anecdotes about kids coming back drunk to the hotel, or stoned from the amusement park after Project Graduation (who the hell came up with *that* idea?), and of course, your basic hooker-in-the-room, blowjobs-at-the-back-of-the-bus-shtick. And I could still recall my own high school Spanish Club trip to Barcelona, where I spent half the night riding around on a moped with a boy named Paulo, oblivious to the hair-tearing, embassy-calling panic I was inspiring back at the hotel. These are things that occur when you take a group of other people's children off school grounds. On the field trip request form you are supposed to list your educational objectives, but who the hell thinks about that? No one. You're too busy praying that everyone makes it through alive, sober, and still a virgin. *These* are the objectives, baby. Lose sight of this and you will be sorry.

Nonetheless, they always want you to come up with some pedagogical crap about what you want the kids to learn from the trip. Christ, you'd think it was obvious. I mean, take my trip to Salem, Mass. We're talking *The Scarlet Letter*, Nathaniel Hawthorne Museum, Salem Witch Trials, seafaring history, transcendentalism, you name it, it's at the Peabody museum. An intoxicating blend of literature and early American history, for God's sake. (Plus, Claire had told me about an amazing tarot card reader there—even better than the chick on Fourth Avenue in Brooklyn). If an administrator had ever read a book, he would know that taking an American Lit class to Salem was a good thing. If they'd had a decent high school education themselves, they wouldn't be asking you why you want to take the kids to Salem. But I seriously doubt a principal ever reads anything except *The One Second Principal*, or *How to Trick New Teachers into Coaching Debate*. I'm just saying.

Being the new girl, however, I dutifully wrote up a one-page, single-spaced essay on the educational merits of a one-day trip to Salem. I was getting pretty excited about going, because I had that new-teacher-desire-to-impress-the-world thing I told you about before. I proofread it twice that night, and sent it to the principal the next day with a sheet of logistical information.

My essay came back at the end of the day with a little green slip attached. These little papers that principals love to attach are never good. The principal does not suddenly look up from his pile of principal papers and say to himself, "By God, that Maura Danner is worth five Ennigers! I think I'll invite her down for a chat about her raise." They only attach a little slip of paper when you've screwed up. This particular little piece of paper read, "Does not match the State Learning Results Standards." So he hadn't read my essay.

Apparently the principal no longer has the good judgement or common sense enough to okay a fairly obvious request for a standard field trip. The State must be involved. So natch, I scuttled off to ask if anyone had a copy of the State Learning Results Standards. Of all people, it was Sully who had it. I took a look at it, and frowned. It was pages and pages of edu-speak, and someone had spent a great many months, now lost forever, writing it.

"This is..." Dismayed, I couldn't find the words.

"Total crap?" Sully said. "Of course it is, kid, but you gotta do it."

"But I don't even know how to read this."

"No one *reads* it. Just say you're complying with standard H-5. That's the one I always use."

I smiled. Thank God for the Silver Fox. "Thanks, Old Man."

Old H-5 did the trick, but to make assurance double sure, I threw in a G-3. The field trip was approved and Sully agreed to come along as a co-chaperone. It turns out that he was a real teacher, he taught American History, so it was a good match. He coached softball and the kids liked him, and I was fairly certain that he could make decent conversation at lunch, which is *key* in a chaperone. I once made the mistake of allowing a parent to come on a field trip, and all day long I heard about her divorce and some bizarre prison case she was involved in. She wanted to pass out a petition to free some homicidal psychopath who had held two nuns and an old dog at gunpoint for hours, but I didn't let her.

The kids, of course, were thrilled that they'd be getting out of the classroom.

"Is Salem in New York? You're always talking about New York."

"How much does it cost?"

"Can I bring my skateboard?"

"What day is that? Is that a Thursday?"

"Will we be tested on this?"

"Ms. Danner, what day is that? Is that a Thursday?"

"Do you dye your hair?"

"What day is that?"

"We leave at 6:30 am sharp. You snooze, you lose," I said.

So at 6:35, Tyler Eaton had still not shown up. (There is always a kid who doesn't show up.) I took the list of kids into the main office, got back on the bus, and we left, despite loud protests from Tyler's entourage, the stoner crowd. From their point of view, it was completely unfair to warn Tyler repeatedly about being late, write it in capital letters on the permission slip, then actually leave without him when he did not show up on time. Most of the class, being teenagers, seemed to agree with Tyler's brat pack, and I could tell we were starting off on the wrong foot. Too damn bad, I thought, we had a schedule and anyway, life without Tyler Eaton was better than life with him. Sully was peacefully reading his newspaper while this exchange occurred, suggesting that he would be as effective as a co-chaperone as he had been a co-chair.

The second mistake I made was the movie. Knowing we had a couple of hours to kill in the early morning, I had selected a PBS docudrama about Nathaniel Hawthorne. This was not well received, and when I turned it off at 8:00 am no one even noticed. (Documentaries in the morning are an acquired taste, I suppose. Now an experienced hand at long bus rides with adolescents, I know that the correct choice is *Mulan*, which instantly makes them sway and sing along to the "I'll Make a Man out of You" number. Seriously, they love it. This is because teenagers are egocentric, and they're weirdly nostalgic about their own childhoods, which happened five minutes ago.)

At 8:15, the shrieking began.

"It's Tyler, Ms. Danner! It's Tyler!"

I staggered to the back of the bus and from the little square window I had a perfect view of Tyler Eaton on a motorcycle, wearing no helmet, zooming along one-handed, waving to his fans. His black hair whipped away from his face, revealing deep set brown eyes, a pointy jaw and a smirk. With his oversized leather jacket and oily jeans he could have passed for a Hell's Angel, or Eddie without the Cruisers.

Jesus God.

I lurched back to the front of the bus and consulted with Sully. Should we pull over? Get him on the bus? What would we do with the motorcycle? Could we just let him follow us?

Was he technically my responsibility, even though he wasn't on the freaking bus? Hell, we had crossed into another state. Could I be fired for this? If you're any good, half of your career will be spent wondering if you can be fired for something, by the way, so this was a natural and correct state of affairs.

We decided, rightly, that there was nothing to be done. He had come of his own accord; as a second time around senior he was certainly old enough to legally drive a motorcycle. The best course of action was to let him follow us to Salem. I was furious, and planned to let him know the moment we got there.

When we got to The Witch Museum, our first stop, I gathered everyone at the doors and did a head count. Tyler said nothing to me, but I noticed him over by the fence, showing Sully the finer points of his engine. Sully was standing with his arms crossed across his chest in an admiring way while Tyler sat on the bike and chatted amiably, occasionally touching the handlebars. Hot tip: do not take field trips with anyone who coaches high school sports. They are too susceptible to juvenile bullshit. They can't help it. Once you get them away from the school, they pretty much act like kids. (Weirdly, sometimes when you take the kids out of school they act like adults, so this might be alright, but you never know. At best, it's risky. What you want, I now know, is a big fat janitor to come with you. They can crush kids with their bare hands.)

Seeing Sully palavering with Tyler Eaton made me lose my nerve. I didn't want to look ridiculous. If you're going to ream out one of the most popular deadbeats in the school, it must be done delicately. I decided to wait for a more opportune moment. The Witch Museum, for the record, is hokey as hell. We got a nifty, politically correct lecture on Wiccan after the dramatization of the story of John and Elizabeth Proctor, complete with a light up devil that elicited appreciative squeals from the girls. The next stop was the House of Seven Gables, and we were to go there on foot. I gave out maps and kids formed their cliques and meandered toward the water.

We had an hour for lunch before we had to actually be at the museum, and I planned to take Tyler aside and give him the what for, but he took off fast with his buddies and I didn't have a chance. It was strangely terrifying to let the kids wander off by themselves, but I had done my research. There wasn't too much trouble to get into in Salem, I thought. Besides, there comes a point on every field trip when you have to let the kids go and just hope they don't commit a felony. Not on your watch, anyway.

My trip came off with only one teeny weeny felony, which I thought was pretty good, since it was my first time.

Museum guides are tricky. A good one has to roll with the punches, and there are always punches when you have fifty kids crammed into a room with five-and-a-half-foot ceilings and priceless antiques. Our guide at the House of Seven Gables was inexperienced. I could tell because she pretty much let us know that she hated the kids. She was a pretty twenty-something with long, curly dark hair and a sharp eye for shenanigans. She stood in front of us with her arms behind her back in the relaxed pose of a soldier. Those guys aren't really relaxed, though—they're just waiting for the right moment to kill you.

"All gum must be thrown away *now*," was her opening line. I was the only one chewing any, so while she passed the adorable little white bucket, I discreetly swallowed it.

Aside from this breakfast that would take seven years for my stomach to digest, everything was going pretty well. The kids loved the secret stairway, and no one touched anything. We were divided into two groups, and mine finished the tour first. While I was ratting around the gift shop, Sully came striding in, his face pale.

"You ready to go?" he asked. "The kids are on the bus."

"Sure," I said, putting the inkwell down. "I was thinking of getting one of these for my classroom, what do you think? I was also considering getting one of those ferrules, which are hilarious." I slapped an imaginary ruler on the palm of my hand and grinned wickedly.

"Great. We gotta get back to the bus."

I noticed how his skin glistened. The man looked like he was going to be sick.

"Are you ok? Was it those burritos? I knew you shouldn't have eaten them. I mean, I think burrito means little donkey in Mexican, which can't be good. We should have had roast beef and figgy pudding or something. You know. Puritan food." I chuckled.

"I broke something and we have to leave. Now, " he whispered.

"You *broke* something?"

"Yes. I stayed behind in that little room and I was looking at a teacup that was on a desk and I dropped it and it broke."

I stared at him. "Why did you pick it up?" I asked stupidly. This was not the most important question to ask, but I was wondering what had motivated him. Maybe Sully, beneath his jockish facade, was a collector of fine porcelain.

Perhaps he enjoyed doilies as well.

"I don't know," he whined tragically. "My wife collects them. I thought this one was the same as one of hers. Can we go now?" He wore the expression of a wet cat.

"Well, did you tell anyone that you broke it?" I was beginning to think it was funny, him breaking a two-hundred-year-old teacup. I was smiling, and I could feel the giggles coming on.

"No. And I'm not going to. Let's go."

"Wait a minute," I said, grabbing him by the sleeve. "You have to tell someone what you did, Sully, or you could get into real trouble." It suddenly occurred to me that we both could. We were chaperones, for Christ's sake. And that teacup could be worth a zillion bucks—I watch Antiques Roadshow. Then something else occurred to me. "What did you do with the pieces?"

"I put the big ones in my pocket, and the rest I kicked behind the door."

"I can't believe this," I said, my tone shifting. I stared at him, calculating how bad this could be. Scenario one: they would stop us at the gift shop door, then take us into a little room with a security guard. Sully would fess up and we'd be fined. The kids would find out and both our reputations would be shot. A parent would complain, it would get into the local paper and

Ms. Danner of the probationary contract would be fired. Scenario two: Sully would confess to the nearest museum employee, probably the old lady at the cash register, and *then* we'd be hauled into the little room, etc. Scenario three: Sully would walk out of the gift shop, we'd get on the bus, we would drive out of the state and no one would ever know. Tempting, but Sully is the kind of man who would have to brag about it to someone, and then everyone would find out and I'd be fired anyway.

"Sully, you have to tell them what you did. They won't send you to prison or anything. You'll just have to cough up the price of the teacup. It probably happens all the time." I tried to sound encouraging.

"No way. They'll find out later and they'll think it was some kid, so we're fine."

I loved how he said "we". What a calculating bastard he was.

"I'll turn you in..." I said, trying to jolly him up, but hoping it would scare him to his senses. This turned out to be a strategic error comparable to running to third instead of first.

His eyes narrowed. "Listen, you arrogant bitch. You do, and I'll see that you don't make it through the year. Do you hear me?" he said in a low staccato. His face was all hard lines. The Silver Fox had turned into a dragon. I was furious, but there wasn't much to say after that; he was right. If I reported the incident no one would believe me. I would look like an insecure new teacher, which I was. Sully had seniority. He was friends with the secretaries. He had the principal's ear. He had a history with the place. I had a few months under my belt.

"Fine!" I hissed. "But this is unbelievable!" Not much of a comeback, but it showed some spunk on my part.

The kids were preoccupied with watching Tyler Eaton pop wheelies behind the bus all the way home, so they didn't seem to notice that Sully and I did not say one word to each other. I fully expected police sirens at any moment—my god, what if they had a video camera in that room?—but nothing happened. We stopped at Burger King and everyone predictably piled out, consumed junk food, then piled back in. Stacy Stanchion tried to get on the back of Tyler's bike, but I put the kibosh on that. When we finally pulled up to the high school driveway at 7 pm, however, the police were waiting. I wasn't sure if they were after Sully (theft) or Tyler Eaton (riding out of state while under the auspices of the school) or me (for "letting" him do it), but did it matter? As the kids piled out of the bus, Sully and I exchanged violent looks. His probably meant "Say one word, Danner, and you die." My own scared rabbit face clearly communicated that I would keep mum unless they pried the truth out of me with pliers.

As I stepped off the bus, a cop approached and said, "Was there an Earl Becker on the bus?"

Ruh-roh. "Yes."

Perhaps Mrs. Eugene Becker had finally died. I hoped Earl wouldn't take it to hard. Who else did he have in this world, besides those budgies? For a moment I considered adopting him.

"Could you point him out, please?"

That was easy. He was lurking by the school doors, alone as always, his head tilted in that strange, listening pose, as if Freddie Mercury were close by.

"He's the kid in the suit. Is something wrong?"

The policeman took me by the arm and led me into the lobby, while another officer escorted Earl. I was just about to scream "EARL DIDN'T BREAK THE TEACUP! MR. SULLIVAN DID!" when Mr. Laverdiere opened the door to his office and ushered us all inside. "Earl, we have some information that leads us to believe that you may be concealing a weapon. Son, are you carrying a firearm?"

I looked at Earl, incredulous.

Earl appeared confused. "Well, Mithter Laverdiere, if by firearm you mean thith little pithtol..." he moved his hand toward his jacket pocket and the two cops practically tackled him. One of them pulled out a small revolver and handed it to the other cop, who put it in a plastic bag.

"Loaded," announced the officer with the plastic bag.

"Earl...what the *fuck*?" was all I could think of to say. Not very professional, but people, I'd had a long day.

"Mith Danner ith innothent," Earl stated calmly, as the officers handcuffed him. "And," he added slyly, "she ith an *exthellent* teacher!"

After they'd taken Earl away in the cop car, Laverdiere explained to Sully and me that they had received a call from Mrs. Becker that morning, shortly after we'd left for Salem, tipping them off to the fact that Earl might have stolen her handgun. She didn't know why. (No one questioned why a 90-year-old woman had a handgun, but whatever...) I could imagine why Earl had stolen it, though—some elaborate film noir fantasy he was reconstructing in his head probably required it. Or perhaps he was re-enacting "Bohemian Rhapsody": *Mamma, just killed a man, put a gun against his head, pulled the trigger, now he's dead...* Earl's world was pretty logical, if you dared explore it.

"So let me get this straight. All day long while I was running around Salem with fifty kids, you suspected one of them was carrying a loaded gun, and it never occurred to you to call and tell me that? Or at least call the cops in Salem? What kind of amateur operation are you running here, you moron? Do you realize what could have happened if Earl had chosen to shoot someone? He's out of his mind, you know, and he's very touchy. But of course, you *don't* know, because you don't know jack shit about any of the kids in this school. You're too busy holing up in your creepy little office writing stupid little memos. Have you ever HEARD of Columbine, you incompetent bastard?"

Did I use quotes just now? Because I didn't actually say this. I thought it, of course, and you are probably thinking it right now, but believe it or not, the magnitude of Laverdiere's stupidity did not occur to me until later, when I was back at my house, safe in the bathtub. Why hadn't the man simply called me, or alerted the Salem police, who could easily have apprehended Earl? The more I thought about it, the angrier I became. I thought of calling my father, because even at twenty-seven when bad stuff happens and you get scared you want Daddy, of course, but I knew my father would barrel down the highway and murder Laverdiere with his own two hands. So instead, I got out of the tub and stormed off to my desk, dripping wet, to write a memo of my own. Thank God for Mrs. Harris, who taught me in 6th grade never to write a letter when you're mad. I hacked away at my computer until I'd had my say, which included a demand for a modest, six-figure settlement for mental distress, Laverdiere's immediate resignation and psychological treatment for Earl Becker, then I deleted it and went to bed.

Here's the bottom line on taking other people's kids out of the school environment and into the wild: You are out there alone, flappin' in the wind. If things go wrong, you cannot count on your administrators to back you. If some kid pulls a gun on you, the only thing that might save you is if you have a good relationship with that kid. You know, if Earl Becker *had* decided to go postal that day, I'm pretty sure he wouldn't have shot me. I don't know for sure, and I never will, but I'm pretty sure he wouldn't have.

But like I said, never underestimate the weird kid.

How to Outsmart the Crisis Plan and Live to Teach Another Day

Shame on me. All this talk of guns, and I haven't told you about the Crisis Plan yet. Every school is supposed to have one, so if a wack job with an AK-47(or Earl Becker) shows up you know what to do. Ours involves a lot of crouching, whispering and hiding. If an intruder comes in, and if he doesn't shoot the secretaries before they have time to get on the PA and say "Code Red," we're supposed to lock our doors, pull down the shades, turn out the lights, and hide around the corner, out of sight of the Evil One with A Gun. My trailer was in the back parking lot of the school, which meant I was a sitting duck, basically. The two windows at the back of the trailer had no shades. They were supposed to have them, but someone didn't put in for them so Ozzie, the janitor, helped me hang up two opaque Felix the Cat shower curtains instead. From inside, I could look out across the fields to a wood where the kids smoked pot. From outside, unless the person looking in stood right behind the the profile of Felix (highly unlikely), he could see into the classroom. So the shooter could walk past, look in those windows and there we'd be, crouching in the corner like cats trying to hide behind a penny.

I know, I know. It's insane, but if you teach high school you have to figure it'll happen eventually, because it happens every year in the good ole USA. Like it or not, school shootings have become an occupational hazard, like concussions to a football player, yet another reason they are *really* not paying you enough. I have a friend who began her teaching career at an elementary school in Los Angeles. The very first hour of her very first day as a teacher, a student shot the principal. The shooter was in second grade. She did not go running back to her corporate America job, either, by the way. She stayed because she was the third kind of teacher, and she was tough as nails. Some of those kindergarten teachers are made of iron, man. I'm just sayin'.

So you try to sound nonchalant as you explain to the kids that yeah, we need to stop talking about Dickens and prepare for our imminent violent deaths—*again*. The thing is, it's always a kid who comes rambo-ing in with a semi-automatic, and the kids *know* that everyone is hiding around the corner. Still, we go through the motions, and there are a couple of pointers to keep in mind.

First of all, if the alarm goes off when you

are on a free period, do what you're supposed to do, or you will find yourself, as I did my first time, embarrassed. My buddy Jennifer and I got caught in the teacher's lounge having a warm cuppa while the rest of the school was standing outside in the rain, going through an absurd evacuation drill that would certainly have resulted in mass casualties had it been a real emergency, but that's beside the point. Laverdiere came into the room, probably looking for a warm cuppa himself, the bastard, and found us all cozy and chatting on the couch.

"You two are supposed to be outside, helping with the evacuation," was all he said.

"Isn't that what *you're* supposed to be doing?" I said in a cartoon bubble over my head. "Yes, Sir," I said out loud. Jennifer and I scuttled out to the cold drizzly parking lot, where the whole school saw our humiliation.

"Busted," Sully whispered as we walked by.

"F You," Jennifer shot back, which is why she was my friend.

You really have to watch the kids when all twenty-five of you are squished into the corner of the room breathing on each other. You're supposed to keep them quiet while the cops walk around and rattle the doors to see if they're really locked. This is relatively easy for the first five minutes, then it's not so easy. There's the usual squirming, and some kids try to use their cell phones to text kids in the next room, that kind of thing. In my case, Tyler Eaton tried to have sex with Mandy Jones in the corner. I stopped them, natch. (That's the thing about kids. No discretion.)

It is sometimes useful to keep a button and a long piece of string handy. A button had fallen off my cheap-ass teacher shirt from Target (I stapled it together), and there was still a roll of string in my desk from some project or other. To pacify the natives, I made a huge circle of string, and put the button on it, so it could slide around. We all held the string, and hid the button with our hands as we sent it skittering around, and took turns guessing who had it. Believe it or not, this kept them occupied for quite a while.   In fact, we were having such a raucous time with Who's Got the Button that an hour went by and we were still there, quietly giggling. Finally Earl said, "Mith Danner, are you sure thith ith a drill?"

It had been a while, and the drill should have been over. I stuck my neck out and looked up at the clock. It was almost 2:10—the busses would be leaving at 2:15. I didn't hear anything, but my classroom was in the trailer at the back of the school, so I never heard anything. Why hadn't the school police officer come to tell me to unlock the doors and go back to teaching as usual? During a drill, we're not supposed to use the phone, or even answer it if it rings. We're not supposed to step foot outside the classroom, or look out a window. We're just supposed to wait there, like sitting ducks, and hope that our tiny town in the middle of nowhere has a state-of-the-art SWAT team.

So we waited, and then Mandy said, "It's two-fifteen, Ms. Danner. I gotta go get my bus." She started to get up.

"Sit down!" I hissed at her. "The drill's not over."

"It is too," drawled Tyler.

"I gotta work," Mandy whined.

"No you don't," I snapped. "We have to stay here until they come get us." I'd already been busted by Laverdiere for not complying once, this time I was determined to get it right.

"Thith ith not a drill." We all looked at Earl.

"Shut up, Becker," said Tyler.

I have never been good in a crisis, as you will recall from the last professional crisis I told you about, and when you're suddenly responsible for other people's children, a bizarre form of adrenaline takes over. A couple of nervous kids looked at me quickly. Perhaps they were recalling how Earl had been a bit of a sniper himself on my Salem trip. Hopefully, he was taking his meds today.

"We're just going to stay right here, until Officer Santoni comes and gets us," I said calmly.

"What if he's dead?" said Hannah, a quiet kid. 'What if they're *all* dead?" Hannah wanted to be an actress. Her IEP stated that she was allowed to get up and spontaneously leave the room if she needed to, but I hoped she wouldn't remember that. "I mean, why else would he not come? If he were alive, he'd have come by now."

Suddenly we were in a Stephen King novel. Yes, that's right, I wanted to say, everyone in the universe is dead except our little class and the killer, and it's up to us to save the planet, from the trailer. And then I thought, hey—that might be a pretty good movie premise. I started to cast it in my head. Ok, I would of course be the lead, and George Clooney....

"Do you hear that?" said Andy Holland, the super smart kid who never said anything but wrote excellent essays. "It's a helicopter. That's the FBI, I bet."

If another kid had said it, Tyler Eaton would have told him to shut up and that would have been the end of it. But Andy never said anything that wasn't brilliant, so we all crouched there, listening for the approaching sound of whirring blades.

"Oh my God, this is real," said Hannah.

"Thith ith tho exthiting."

"Ms. Danner, should we do something? Go somewhere? Like, out the window? Then we could run into the woods," Andy suggested. He looked at me with almost, shall I say it, contempt. So now our *Lord of the Flies* roles were coming out. Andy was definitely Jack, the megalomaniacal choir boy, which meant he had to be squashed.

"No, we're going to stay put until they come and get us," I said firmly. I was definitely Ralph, the humanist and hero of the novel. And Earl, of course, made a perfect Piggy, the scapegoat. It's nuts, but English teachers are like this. In a crisis, we cast ourselves in disaster movies and figure out which *Lord of the Flies* character we are. That's how we know what to do.

"If there is an intruder, we can't let him know that we're here," I said robotically.

"I'm going to just look out the window," whispered Andy. He was too far away for me to grab him and stop him, so we all watched him slither on his belly to the other side of the room, stand up, quickly slip under the shower curtain and look out, then drop down to the floor again. A moment later he crawled back to our side of the room.

"The coast is clear," he whispered seriously. "We could make it to the woods."

"This is bullshit," Tyler Eaton offered.

All the kids looked at me. I knew what we were supposed to do. We were supposed to stay hidden until the officer came and told us the coast was clear. I considered the possibilities. Either they were goofing on us, or there really was someone out there with a gun. I was responsible for these kids. Even the kids I didn't like. Would I actually have to take a bullet for Deirdre, the nose-picker? I remembered what had happened on the Salem trip. How they hadn't told me that we were all in danger. Maybe that was happening again. I wouldn't put it past them.

Just then there was an enormous bang coming just outside the door. Jesus—was that a gunshot? I didn't know what a gun sounded like. It might have been something in the main building, how would I even know what craziness what going on over there? I suddenly realized that we were all alone in the trailer. No one could get to me; they'd all be hunkered down in their own rooms back in the main building. There was another loud bang, and then someone rattled the door handle. This was the moment when I saw what really goes on in a crisis. A couple of girls screamed and then the gig was up—we were found out—we'd blown our own cover and we all leapt up and ran like lemmings to the window. Andy tore Felix the Cat down, and the curtain rod bounced off his head. He thrashed his way through the riot of smiling plastic cat and flung open the window. In an instant the kids were shoving each other through it like you shove clothes into a suitcase.

"Get out! Get out!' I shrieked, jumping up and down. I was herding the kids through the window, not caring what happened to them afterward. The only thing that mattered was getting far away from that door. Thank God Tyler Eaton kept his head and opened up the other window, and kids started clambering through that one. I wanted all the kids to get out first, but I also wanted them to get the hell out of the way so *I* could get out first. It was the most terrifying twenty seconds of my life.

Finally it was my turn to get out, so I kicked off my kitten heel pumps, hiked up my skirt and hoisted my foot onto the window ledge when I heard the door again. The sniper was trying to get inside the room! Jesus God, he was going to shoot the door down! I jumped forward and fell on the open window sill and started frantically squirming. The pain on my stomach was agony, but I didn't care.

A moment later Ozzie the janitor opened

the door with his key and came inside, looking like Jackie Gleason dragging a huge metal trash bin. Banging it, actually.

"Maura, what are you *doin'*?" he asked.

At the sound of his voice I stopped trying to get out the window and let myself slump back into the room. I turned and stared at him stupidly.

"We heard a noise..." I trailed off. Outside the kids were streaking across the grass into the woods, yelling and waving their arms. My stomach felt as it had been stapled to my knees.

"Oh my Lord, did they forget about you, honey?" he said. "Didn't they come and get you?"

Nope. They did not.

Luckily for *moi*, no one had been seriously hurt in the mad dash to escape Ozzie the janitor. I could have strangled Andy Holland for his panicky leadership, but I decided to play it cool, as if I wasn't embarrassed at all, as if I'd planned it, just to see what they'd do. The next day I was marginally famous with the moms in the supermarket for my "heroics" —getting those poor traumatized kids out before myself, which was actually me screwing up the instructions to stay put, but no one seemed to remember that. At school I was the butt of many a joke, and Laverdiere avoided me for several days

171

afterward, because he knew he'd screwed up. My only compensation for the utter humiliation was to discover that when the shit hits the fan, in the *Lord of the Flies* analogy, I am Ralph.

Sometimes the drill is real though, and *then* things get interesting. Along with the sniper debacle, my first year there was also a bomb scare. There I was, teaching the pants off of Walt Whitman, when all of a sudden the announcement comes over the PA for the whole school to evacuate the building. We're supposed to go out and get on a bus—any bus—and then we all get taken to some safe place. In our case, it was a large gymnasium at the middle school. The first great thing about that day was that I was on the same bus as Jennifer. We taught a lot of the same kids that year, and a lot of them were on the bus with us, since they'd just come from Jenn's class. So it was pretty cozy, lots of in jokes and goofing around as the bus trolled along to the middle school. The kids were psyched—they got out of a biology quiz *and* they might get to see the school blow up.

When we got to the middle school, everyone piled out of the bus and strolled into the gymnasium, where there were already about a thousand other kids and teachers waiting there. There was a strangely festive atmosphere, as if we were going to have a pep rally.

Teachers were clustered together in the middle of the enormous space, talking, and the kids had broken off into their own social niches and were contentedly chattering. I stood around with Jennifer and Stephanie and Pauline and discussed Pauline's husband's birthday party. Jenn wanted to know if Pauline was going to hire a stripper for the guy, and we had fun with that for quite a while.

As the minutes wore on, people began to sit down in little groups on the gymnasium floor, talking or playing cards. It's against the rules to play cards in most schools, but the kids, weirdly prim, were playing Old Maid, so we didn't say anything.

After a couple of hours went by, people started getting hungry. No one had told us what was going on, if there really had been a bomb, or when we'd be taken back to the high school. We were only told that we could not leave the gym. So we sat around and played cards, and after a while we began to forage for food.

"I've got a pack of gum," offered Mallory and she quickly distributed the pieces to the kids in our circle. She came up about five pieces short.

"Oh no, that's ok," said Jack, a scrawny freshman. "I'll go without."

"No—rip them in half!" Mallory instructed

dramatically.

"Yes, make sure everyone gets one," said someone else.

It was weird. I mean, these were the kids I hoped would be on the Titanic 2 with me someday. They were so freaking nice to each other. They got a huge kick out of dividing the spoils, as Mallory called it. "Let no man starve," she said, as she ripped each piece gleefully in half. There was a lovely feeling of Aren't Bomb Scares Fun, and slowly the barriers between teacher and student were breaking down.

"I found a tic tac!" squealed Jennifer, as she pulled a moldy little blue thing up from the depths of her pocket.

"Let's split it!" I said, laughing.

Truth be told, though, I was getting pretty hungry, and a tic tac was not going to do it for me. Not to mention the fact that teenage boys are sharks; they need to feed every hour. It was already 11:30, two hours past my lunch time. The kids were getting quiet, probably because they were weak from hunger. When the vice principal told us we might have to be there another couple of hours because they had to search every single inch of the high school and all the cars in the parking lot, Jennifer decided that we needed to order take-out.

"Excellent idea, Jennster," I said, then

realized that I didn't have any money because I didn't have any purse. First rule of evac drills: *always* grab your keys and your purse. It turns out no one had any money except the kids.

Our circle on the gym floor had become a lifeboat, and the kids quickly rallied, pooling their cash in the middle. We had a total of $5.74, not even enough for one pizza.

Here's where the wind shifted. Mike McMahon, one of my seniors, stood in the center of the gym and lifted his cellphone in the air.

"I just called Waller's," he announced. "They said they will donate some pizzas!" Man, I thought, that kid should run for office. He was better than Giuliani after 9/11. The kids who'd heard him started cheering. Still, we had over five hundred students and fifty or so faculty. Wallers was generous, but it wouldn't be enough. Then Carrie, whose husband owned a restaurant in town, informed us that he was bringing over a huge tray of sandwiches.

"My mom is coming with some leftovers!" a kid announced.

"My dad is bringing some meatloaf sandwiches," added another.

Soon the whole gymnasium was glowing with good intentions, as kids called home for supplies. Parents showed up and kids greeted them at the doors, then distributed the food. The local supermarket produced several huge jugs of water. Mike McMahon was still on his cellphone, probably talking to Obama.

A couple of kids I didn't know came up to the vice principal and asked if they could go to the school library. A few minutes later they came back and started setting up a laptop and a projector to show a movie. Next thing I know, Mike McMahan, Mayor of the Middle School Gym, was ushering in a man carrying about a hundred buckets of popcorn from the local tenplex. Damn, I should have thought of that! Another couple of minutes later, the whole school was sitting on the floor, munching on popcorn and looking up at a watery projection of *Mulan* on enormous red velvet curtains. (What *is* it about high school kids and that movie?) As the whole student body started singing "I'll Make a Man Out of You," even Michael Penny, the extremely autistic kid, was rocking and smiling like crazy, holding onto his aide's hand. I knew that he felt it too, this spontaneous camaraderie. For the first time he looked like he was having a great time, like he was really part of the school.

The bomb scare ended before *Mulan* did, but the kids were good about throwing their trash in the bins, and getting back on the busses. As we rode back to the high school I could feel the energy fading, the more mundane attitudes and behaviors coming back. It didn't matter, though. Bread had been broken and friendships had been forged. Aside from the fact that we live in a world where sick people like to blow up innocent children, the bomb scare was by far one of the best days of the year.

Truman Capote and the Love Class

There is something magical about the first year teaching, even though you are at your worst. You bring an energy to the classroom that you will never be able to harness again in quite the same way. It's like trying out a new recipe and screwing it all up, and having it come out wonderful anyway. Try to make the same mistakes again, and you can't, because it wasn't skill, it was luck. If you're really lucky your first year, you'll get a Love Class, and that's what makes you want to do it all again the next September.

The Love Class doesn't come along very often, but when it does, teaching is like sitting around with twenty-five of your funniest, best friends who all love the books the way you do. These are the kids you would be friends with if they were your age. They get your humor, they love to play, they read the hell out of everything you throw at them. Sometimes they're even more fun to be with than your real friends.

The second semester of my first year, I was wildly lucky and got my first Love Class, although I didn't *know* it was a Love Class then.

These seniors were so fun and so smart that when the bell rang kids would actually sigh with disappointment. We'd just finished reading *In Cold Blood*. Cassie had regaled us with a story about how she was reading it while babysitting, and the power went out, and she hid in the closet and cried until the people came home. We were laughing and trading our favorite creepy passages, and then I mentioned that the movie *Capote* had just come out, which is all about how Truman Capote wrote the book and what it did to him psychologically. I rarely show movies in class (HUGE waste of time), but I encouraged them to go see it, and before I knew it, they had convinced me to see it *with* them on Monday night. I was skeptical at first, remembering how that other, Unlove class had stood me up at the Indian restaurant, but the kids were so insistent, and the film would be a fabulous follow up to the novel itself. You know, first the story of the murders, then the story of how the writing of the story changed the way people write. The real reason I let the kids talk me into going to the movies on a freezing cold Monday night in January is that Philip Seymour Hoffman is hot and I have a thing for dead gay writers, but that did not meet any of the State Learning Standards, so I pulled out the old H-5 and G-3 again, which worked like a charm. My little ranch house was on of those in-town back streets, so I agreed to walk over and meet them at the movies, then go to a coffee house afterward for discussion. I didn't like to admit it to myself, but I was really looking forward to hanging out with my kids. (See? See what I just said? "My" kids. This is what the Love Class can do to you.)

The whole class came. They had their permission slips for the R rating and everything. This was going swimmingly. I figured they'd all go sit together on those disgusting couches they have down front, but they all sat in the middle, with me. The cinema was empty except for our gang, and so we could make all the smart-ass comments we wanted, which we did, for the first ten minutes. Once they recovered from Philip Seymour Hoffman's teeny weeny Capote voice, they were riveted. We had read the hell out of Capote's novel, so every scene was perfumed with significance. They loved the film, and we came out into the lobby talking fast and imitating that weird little voice. Giuseppe Bartolo opened the exit doors and yelled back to us, "You guys! It's *snowing*!"

There is nothing kids like more than silent, lovely snow. It always surprises them, and it can convert even the most cynical, jaded sixteen year old into a wide-eyed waif. We all crowded through the door to see and it was indeed magical. While we'd been rapt in front of the silver screen, the town had been transformed into a tiny village in Germany, a snow globe, a Narnian wood. The snow was coming down thickly, our eyelashes were caking with it. We stood for a moment with our faces upturned, licking at the flakes, then we ran down the street to the cafe. When we got there, the windows were forebodingly dark—the sign on the door said in someone's hasty scrawl, "closed due to blizzerd." We laughed at the error, then stood around awkwardly. I'd chosen that coffeehouse because it was the only place in town where kids could be served. Everything else in walking range was a bar, and they all looked closed anyway. In fact, the storm had shut down the whole town. It was a snow day, but at night.

Then I noticed Cassie's feet. Yes, indeed it is true, sometimes kids lack the common sense God gave the ant. She was barefoot.

"Cassie, where are your shoes?" I said.

"In my car."

Ah, if I had a dollar for every time a kid said *that*.

"And where's your car?"

"In my driveway." Christ, she was such a blonde.

The snow was falling so hard our tracks were already covered. The kids' parents weren't supposed to get them for at least an hour. I had to make a decision or Cassie's feet were going to fall off.

"Ok. We'll go to my house," I heard myself say.

I must pause and tell you do not try this at home. Never invite kids into your lair, your den, your happy place. They'll crap all over it and ruin it. They'll suck the joy out of it and leave a mess behind. Invade your personal space. Violate your privacy. Disrespect the fine line between Teacher and Real Person. They'll rip the mojo to shreds and piddle on the carpets. They will see the embarrassing photo of you when you had braces and wore high waters and that gross patent-leather belt. This was true, this I knew for sure, but I did it anyway, because of Cassie's feet.

One kid, Paul Anderson, had his own car and bailed, which turned out to be the equivalent of Pete Best leaving the Beatles, but no one knew it yet.

As we trudged two blocks through the blizzard to my house, I did a mental tally. Did I leave my underwear drying on the radiator? Were the kitchen counters gooey? What if a kid asked to use the bathroom? Would he go through my medicine closet and find something scandalous? Where *did* I put that picture of me in the high waters? Where would I even put all those freaking kids? What if things got weird, and no one wanted to have a discussion, and we all sat around the kitchen table saying nothing for a whole hour? What if they really didn't want to talk about the movie at all, but wanted to go get high in the basement? I felt strangely shy, like I was on a first date with twenty-four teenagers.

At least my street did look charmingly Dr. Zhivago-esque in the snow, I thought, as we all crunched up my front steps. We slapped our arms and banged our toes against the steps and came inside. Thank God I have a long, wide hallway, and a lot of pegs on the wall for coats. Old Jukes the Cat came around the corner, saw all those kids taking off their shoes in the hallway, and took off into the dark Netherlands under the bed.

That was the first wonderful thing—they took off their shoes. I didn't even have to ask them. Everyone was suddenly on his best behavior. They slowly made their way into the living room, looking all around at my things awkwardly. Finally one of the girls said "Wow. You have a really nice house," and everyone murmured in agreement. I didn't have a really nice house back then, it was a crappy ranch like I told you, but they were setting the mood, putting me at ease.

Feeling like a nervous hostess, I zipped into the kitchen waving my arms around in what I hoped was a casual manner and called out, "I have nothing to offer you but Saltines." It was true, I hadn't gone shopping, I was a marm living on a teacher salary in a ranch house, for Chrissakes. They were lucky I had Saltines, or I'd be offering them Friskies, which is something Claire and I had always wanted to try at a party, you know, to see if anyone noticed. We figured if we poured Friskies into a really pretty glass bowl and set it on the table with the food, some shmuck would try it. Somehow that did not seem appropriate here, so I grabbed the box of crackers from the cupboard and stood into the doorway to the living room.

My Christmas tree was still up, and one of the kids had turned on the lights. The room was simply...aglow. There were kids everywhere—it was like that scene in 101 Dalmatians, where the whole apartment is coated in puppies. Four girls were perched like sparrows to my sofa, three kids occupied the rocking chair and the arm chairs, two hovered in the doorway, five were sitting on the floor, around the coffee table. Three skinny boys had squished themselves onto my piano seat ("Hey, I played that same minuet in fourth grade, Ms. Danner..."), four kids

184

were leaning against the bookshelves by the radiator, and three were in the process of stepping gingerly over everyone else to try and find a spot in front of the tree.

All I can tell you is that my house never felt so much like my house. I stood there with the Saltines in my right hand, and my left hand sort of pointing to them like a TV spokesperson, and we all cracked up. The bay window behind the couch looked dark and mysterious and outside the falling snow lent a cozy intimacy to the room. Jenna reached over to turn on a table lamp and the whole room burst into protest, which was the second wonderful thing.

"No! We just want the Christmas lights! Turn it off!"

They had an intuitive grasp that something extraordinary was about to happen, and the lighting was essential. It was out of my hands—we would talk by twinkling tree.

"Ok, ok, chill already. It's off," Jenna said meekly.

"So," I said, when I had plucked my way to the last bit of available carpet. It was quiet for a moment. "Pass the Saltines."

The atmosphere really was a little like the cabin of Joseph Conrad's boat, with one lantern swinging back and forth, and men trading tales of their first sea voyage and sharing a bottle of rum. No one got the reference, because we hadn't read "Youth" yet, but they nodded appreciatively, almost solemnly, and they passed around that stupid box of Saltines and each kid took one cracker, like it was a communion wafer or something. And then the third really wonderful thing happened. Mallory said quietly, "Ms. Danner, can we start by reading Perry's confession aloud?"

I hadn't thought of reading aloud, but the mood was right, we were all settled in and we wanted a story. Mallory pulled out her copy of *In Cold Blood* and thumbed through it until she found the part where Perry Smith finally confesses to the gruesome details of multiple homicide.

"'*So Dick was afraid of me? That's amusing. I'm very amused. What he don't know is, I almost did shoot him.' Dewey lights two cigarettes, one for himself, one for the prisoner. 'Tell us about it, Perry...'*"

Her reading was so soft that we had to be very quiet to hear it, but it was skillful and well-paced, and the effect was mesmerizing. No one made a peep while she read twenty pages of gorgeous Capote sentences out loud. We were so rapt, that when the doorbell rang we collectively jumped. I scrambled to my feet and answered it. Jimmy Chelius's mom was there to collect him, but we were just getting to the *really* scary part, and Jimmy didn't want to leave, so I motioned for her to come in and she hovered in the doorway while Mallory kept reading. No one moved, except to very, very gently and silently, nibble on a corner of a Saltine.

The doorbell rang again, and again, and a few more times, and pretty soon there were about ten parents standing in the hallway with their coats on, listening. My house now had thirty-four people in it. No one fidgeted, no one got up to go. The parents who couldn't squeeze in to see all the kids in squatting in my tree-lit living room were politely shushed by the parents who could, and so we finished those terrifyingly gorgeous pages. We listeners were holding our breaths in wonder, because this was *Capote*, as Capote himself had intended it.

You can't always plan how things are going to go. Sometimes the best teaching happens at night, in a blizzard. Just think: If it hadn't started to snow and if Cassie hadn't been such a dumbass kid with no shoes and if I had decided not to let my students see my crappy house …we might never have heard Mallory read. We might never have known how absolutely beautifully Mallory can read.

The Holy Effing Grail of Teaching

I don't know about you, but for me, all great revelations happen at The Glorious Golden Chopstick on Mott Street in Manhattan. It's a cheesy, grimy little place with red leather booths and greasy plastic tabletops and it's where Claire and I did all our truth-telling back in the day. And so it was, that while I was finishing up my Masters degree so I could begin my glorious, golden teaching career, Claire said something that stopped me dead in my teacher tracks.

We were talking about how everything was going to change when I got a job and left New York. We knew it was the end of an era-- our era--and we dreaded it because we were addicted to each other's company, and now Claire was going to have to order the Shu-Shu-Shumai Dumplings without me. Although Claire is absolutely brilliant, she's pretty much stunted emotionally, and my looming departure was really bugging her. So maybe that's what made her do it, I don't know, but out of the blue she said, "Well, you sure picked a sucky time to be a teacher."

I looked up, shut my mouth, and put down the shumai. "What's that supposed to mean?"

"It means," she said, twirling her chopstick in the air, "that it is a sucky time to become an English teacher. Nobody reads anymore."

"You LOVE reading." I was starting to feel that horrible, slimy sensation of a difficult truth about to be told.

"Correction," she said, jabbing her chopstick at me. "I DID love to read. Graduate school pretty much ruined that for me." She didn't mean it, and I knew that, but it was all happening, baby, and I couldn't stop it.

"Well, *other* people still read. Just because it's 1993 does not mean that the book is dead," I shot back.

"No, but you won't be able to teach half the stuff you love because the kids don't read," she practically screamed at me. "Words, words, words--they don't know words! And no one even *cares* anymore. I was just reading in the Times that there are these things called emojis, and..."

I cut her off. "Well, Ralph Waldo would disagree with you."

"Uh-oh," Claire said in her snotty voice, "here we go with your Emerson crap. What did the man with the worst hair in history say *this* time?"

"He said "Ours is a very good time, if we but know what to do with it,'" I replied a little too quickly. I sounded like the pedant I was, and for the next few minutes there was only the sound of clinking wood on porcelain.

"Keep telling yourself that, Danner. But the study of literature is pretty much obsolete."

God, I hated her at that moment, because I knew she was right. She was always right.

Click, click, scrape. Finally Claire broke the silence.

"Fuck Emerson," was all she said.

By the time I got home and threw my coat on the couch I was panicking. Oh my God: I was irrelevant, and I hadn't even gotten my degree so I could be *officially* irrelevant! The Museum of Natural History would soon have a new diorama in a dusty, forgotten corner: North Americanus English Teacher at Desk, circa 21 Century. Extinct.

Every English teacher worth her fountain pen has to grapple with the inanity of teaching the value of the written word at some point. And it is much worse for you, Young Ones. What do you think Ole Claire would say if I were, like you, just starting out now, 2016? Parents don't even say "Use your words" anymore--they say, "Use your emojis!" And this goes way beyond the fact that those stupid little frozen smiley faces have replaced "jubilant," "exultant," and "ecstatic." Your whole anti-intellectual world is designed to get you to not have to think about words, or anything, really. The only verbs you need now are click, like, tweet and share. There are almost no bookstores any more, and the ones still kickin' have more greeting cards and puffer balls than actual books. The library has more screens than spines. Current pedagogy--which is supposed to encourage deep thinking and reasoning-- encourages teachers to get kids to write blogs! write scripts! make a power point! watch the movie! do anything except develop a complex idea using language!

Conversely, and here is where it messes with your head, we've still got that ole S.A.T., which is not about blogs, movies, power points or scripts. It's all about understanding how writers have used language to express complex ideas. But you don't want to justify your professional existence by the College Board, right? So that's is not going to cut it.

And anyway, the S.A.T. is not about narrative. We're talking nonfiction, my friends. "Informational text" is the educational quiche of the 2000's. Apparently, what today's kids need is to be able to understand a graph (really? I haven't looked at one since high school), or understand an article on traffic patterns in Detroit. To hell with Mrs. Dalloway and Madame DeFarge! No one reads fiction, we are told--but everyone is going to *have* to learn how to DVR that episode of "The Office", which means reading the manual. Well, reading the instructions on the screen anyway. Even the best teachable contemporary fiction, I'm thinking Donna Tartt's *The Goldfinch*, is instantly corrupted into film before the kids get a chance to experience the prose. And since most teenagers don't watch "Downton Abbey," from now on the deeper truths about life, the kind that *only* come from art, will have to come from "Family Guy."

Turns out Claire *was* right. I did pick a sucky time to become a teacher, but you, my friend, have picked an even suckier one.

So that leaves Ye Who Teach Language Arts (I actually prefer that moniker to "English Teacher," which suggests ye olde Kleenex up the sleeve) in a bit of a shit storm.

Darlings, you are going to have to come to grips with this. You are going to have to develop your own rationalization for why you chose a charming but obsolescent profession, and it had better be good, because at the rate we're going in another ten years there will be no English Teachers any more. (I allude to E.A. Robinson's poem "The Mill" to make myself clear here, but you young ones haven't read it, because we *really* don't teach poetry any more. Still, you get my drift.)

But wait! Some of you are going to insist that there is a way! You do believe in books, you do believe in books, you do, you do, you do, you do, you DO believe in books!

Well, except in the case of *The Wizard of Oz,* whose film version is much better than the book, which is bizarre, I believe in books, too. And after many long conversations with Claire and many, many sake martinis, I figured out why I wanted to leave the greatest city in the world to teach a lost, irrelevant art to an indifferent public for virtually no money and even less prestige. It wasn't easy, but I did it, and you can, too. When you start to feel irrelevant, just:

Step 1: Find your own holy effing grail. If you're gonna do this this right, first you have to decide what the most important thing in life really is. Me, I soul-searched the Beatles, *foie gras,* miniature poodle pups, Agnes B dresses, the New York skyline at night, a fresh hot bagel at H & H, Alan Rickman in *Truly, Madly, Deeply,* the Coliseum, Fred Astaire, that lake house Claire and I rented that one time, and for me, it finally came down to....

Being able to read Shakespeare. Yes, I thought, if kids can do that, I thought, they will have a good life. There's a reason why all those POW's don't ask for a miniature poodle. Or even Alan Rickman. What they cling to in those dark, dank oubliettes….is poetry. Friends will come and go, lovers will disappoint you, and even your dog will up and die on you, but a great read is always there, always faithful, ever panting, forever young, and it always understands you just as you want to be understood.

So after this long mental struggle, I committed to the idea that beauty was in fact really all kids need to know. If you teach science, maybe Einstein's theory of relativity is all kids need to know, or if you teach history, maybe if kids can really understand the Russian Revolution, you'll be able to sleep at night. Whatever you teach--you have to start out knowing that it is the most important thing in the world. It is your holy effing grail, man.

At this point, if you are an English teacher and you do NOT think that being able to read Shakespeare is the most important thing in the world, or at least *one* of the most important things, you may need to reconsider your choice to join this charming, obsolescent profession after all. Go back to start. Do not collect $200. (But reread chapter one.) Because you will never make it.

Step 2: Ask yourself, what's the biggest obstacle to obtaining your holy effing grail? I asked myself what would stand in the way of every kid in America being able to read

Shakespeare, and the answer, of course, was that Shakespeare is freaking HARD. I mean, let's face it, it's out of range for most people, and that's a huge problem. As I sit here writing this in 2016, it's becoming even more out of range. Nowadays most people get around that by just "appreciating" Shakespeare. Instead of studying it, they can just:

a) watch *Shakespeare in Love*. Great movie, a wonderful supplement to reading Shakespeare, but not the same as reading Shakespeare.

b) go to a play. I mean, Shakespeare is meant to be performed, not read, right? Yeah, ok, go ahead and set up your blanket in the park for *Hamlet from a Food Truck*--you might get the general gist of it along with a few mosquito bites, but that's only because you grew up watching *Mister Magoo Does the Classics*, or *WishBone,* or that one *Gilligan's Island* episode where they turned Hamlet into a musical. You probably won't understand a bleeping thing, and even if you do catch a few oft quoted lines and nod smugly to the person on the next blanket, you're not really experiencing Shakespeare, you're experiencing a *Gilligan's Island* re-hash. Now go in your corner and think about that.

c) kid themselves that because Shakespeare's plays are so universal, so relatable, they shouldn't have to work so hard to get it. Ole Billy wouldn't have *wanted* kids to pore over every pun and belabor those lovely lines. Don't be a snob, Danner! Ok, ok, but if you don't look up every word and try to puzzle it out, but how can those words be relatable? How can you appreciate Ophelia's line, "The glass of fashion and the mold of form, Th' observed of all observers" if you have no effing idea what she's talking about? (I know I'm saying "effing" a lot. I'm trying to clean up my language.)

So watching a Gwyneth Paltrow movie, going to see a play, and skipping over any challenging or poetic parts (which means all of it): that's pretty much what most teachers do with Shakespeare. Then they tell themselves oh well, at least I exposed the kids to it. This is Ye Olde Crap, because the real pleasure of watching *Hamlet from a Food Truck* is when you understand what they're saying because you've studied those lines and you've struggled with those soliloquies and you *have* connected it to your own life, because of course it really IS relatable. Shakespeare is like a really great bottle of wine--his language is a 2005 Chateau Lafite Rothschild; there are layers and layers of beauty to behold and drink in.

But you have to be taught how to drink it well.

And you do not chug it from a styro foam cup.

Step 3: Get a plan. Now that my mission was clear--get kids to read and love Shakespeare--and now that I had figured out the challenges before me--basic illiteracy--I had to come up with all the stuff that needed to happen to make that possible. First, I figure they needed to have some Elizabethan vocabulary. Actually, they needed to have a richer vocabulary in general, since the average teen today has five words ("ratchet", "noice", "sup", "sick", and "literally"), so my classes would have to include a lot of memorizing vocab. This would become a constant, daily shout down, and I would have to make it fun.

After looking over that scene in *Macbeth* where Lady Macbeth reads his letter out loud then goes on this pronoun-mad, convoluted speech, I realized that the kids would have to know what a pronoun was, and an antecedent, or they'd never unravel it. In fact, after cruising a few more speeches I realized that the only reason *I* could understand them was not because I possess a brilliant literary mind, but because I could find the main clause, identify the subject, and match up the adjectives and pronouns to the correct nouns. I understood, thanks to my days of French Lit, what a participial adjective was, and I knew that it had to be placed just so in a sentence in order to modify *that* noun and not another noun. I knew that the subject was often five parenthetical asides away from its verb, and that by drawing lines through all the prepositional phrases and subordinate and relative clauses, you could match up that subject to its verb ("Withered murder…blah blah blah…moves like a ghost") and then you could finally get what the hoodle the character was saying.

And all of that, I thought, *can be taught.*

I was starting to feel ok about this charming, obsolescent profession.

Step 4: Stick to the plan, no matter what. Since the entire world was against grammar, books, educational rigor, poetry, making kids struggle a bit, holding them accountable and basically everything that a 19th-century sort of woman like myself holds dear, I knew I would have to take my own measure. Was I prepared to live and teach by my values? You know the TED Talk that has been all over Facebook and at every faculty meeting? The one by Angela Lee Duckworth, where she talks about how success depends not on I.Q. but on grit? Well, if I ever gave a TED talk, I think it would be on how teachers need grit.

If you've ever taught the unteachables (a.k.a. the unbooked), you know that getting them to love a play about a 10th century Scottish dude who goes on and on about a dagger is going to require some serious commitment from you. It's gonna take some grit. Right this moment hundreds of English teachers are giving up on Shakespeare, or reducing it to the AP curriculum. Because what you have to teach in order for a kid to be able to read Shakespeare-- even one soliloquy--is overwhelming.

Which is why we need to get on this thing.

You may not be able to get every kid to understand every word of *Macbeth*, but you can get him to figure out those pronouns in that one speech, which will reveal to his sixteen-year-old mind the absolute deviousness of women, and that is something that, if I had a son, I would want him to know. I would tell that kid that my own beloved husband Charles still to this day has no idea how I got him to remodel the upstairs bathroom. He's still in shock, because he hasn't really read that speech where Lady Macbeth lists all the reasons why Macbeth needs to murder Duncan.

She starts with the fact that he promised he would (total crap), and while he is still trying to recall that conversation she's alluding to, which will be impossible because it never happened, she adds the fact that he must be a real loser if he goes back on his promises, and while he's reeling from that one, she piles on another little gem: she tells him that since he plays so fast and loose with his promises, when he says he loves her, how is she to know whether or not he really means it? (ouch!). She wraps it all up with the ultimate insult: that if he doesn't kill Duncan then he ain't no man worth havin'.

Gentlemen, I hate to say it, but every woman reading this knows that even if we don't pull this stuff, we are capable of it. When I taught *Macbeth* to my own unteachable class, I told them that I had used every trick in the book--this book--to get that bathroom remodeled. And naturally, there was resistance.

Right then ole Travis Cray ups and says in his snotty, creepy, Aryan Nation voice, "You didn't do all that. Women aren't that smart." Of course, I knew that he was suggesting that *I* was not that smart, and I probably would have been left blubbing something about my impressive university degrees, young man, but then the Gods intervened.

There was a knock at the door.

"Whence that knocking?" I said, as I opened the door. It was Mrs. Ruth, the old lady math teacher. They sometimes sent teachers who had a free period out to my trailer with a message for a kid or something.

Here comes the grit.

"Ah, Mrs. Ruth," I said, suddenly and wickedly inspired. "I'm glad you're here. Would you mind telling my students how you get your husband to let you buy things that you want but don't need? You know, like a really expensive shirt that you just can't live without?"

Reader, I kid you not. Without missing a beat, that spunky Mrs. Ruth, who was about three feet tall and sixty-five years old, says, "I just wear it and if he asks about it I would say I've had it for years."

There was an audible gasp from the kids. They sat up.

"And Mrs. Ruth, if I could just detain you for a moment longer," I said, enjoying every moment, "would you happen to have any other strategies for deceiving your husband and getting what you want?"

"Well, I sometimes put the expensive thing in a Walmart bag so when I bring it into the house he thinks I just bought toilet paper or something." She blinked and shifted her feet like a little sparrow, then added, "He never thinks to look in the bag." Math teachers have no sense of humor, so she had no idea how hilarious this was.

A few girls giggled and nodded to each other.

"Oh! And sometimes if he's really pushy," she added, leaning in a bit, "I tell him that my friend Sylvia gave it to me because she didn't want it anymore."

Laughter. I had them now. Even the cynical Travis Cray in the back row, was smiling. He had to admit that there was indeed a secret understanding, an intuition that comes with being female, that Shakespeare got it right. If a nice old teacher lady like Mrs. Ruth pulled this kind of stuff, just think what a PYT could pull off.

The boys looked stunned, the girls looked happy, and I was satisfied. I had hung on, I had not bailed on Shakespeare because it was too hard, I had not given up on the unteachables. I had effing grit! We had slaved over that scene and thanks to Mrs. Ruth, it had paid off. Travis Cray might never understand the entire play, but Shakespeare sure had taught him something about women.

And Reader, don't worry. Claire eventually apologized. Well, that's not exactly true, because Claire *never* apologizes, or explains anything. But she did take me out to a fabulous dinner at a real restaurant before I left town. One without chopsticks.

Be Bloody, Bold, and Resolute

Despite the fact that I just told you how I once invited an entire class into my home, one of the most important skills of teaching is knowing how to establish limits. First of all, do NOT let the kids call you by your first name. You are not on their level, you are not at school to make friends. The trouble is that you're only a few years older than the kids you're teaching, and you look a couple of years younger than some of them, so they see you as an equal. Yes, I know that you think you're all grown-up and worldly because you've been to a couple of frat parties and did a semester in Scotland and all, but really you're still just a kid, and the kids know this.

As a first-year teacher, you're going to have to establish a reputation. This must be done swiftly, and in doing so you must show no fear. If a kid crosses the line, you need to be bloody, bold, and resolute. That's what those apparitions told Macbeth, when he was getting ready to take out Macduff, and you haven't even been seduced by your spouse into murdering your principal yet, so this should work for you first years just fine.

First of all, you need to actually *draw* the

line that the kid has crossed. Mine is currently a strip of red duct tape around my desk. I told the kids they could not cross this line until they were forty.

Still, there are kids who love what they see as a challenge. They will push you right to the edge of sanity every day until you crack. They want to see what you're made of, so you must show them.

In my case, it was that kid I was telling you about, Zachary, who's always touching my stapler. He loved to push my buttons, and every day we did a little dance that was never enough to get him in trouble, but just enough to give me grey hairs. Then on April Fool's day he went way over the line. When I walked into my classroom that fateful morning, everything looked the same... except that every single book of mine was gone. All my Twain, Fitzgerald, Emerson, all my college texts with my annotations—that Balzac novel I'd bought at Shakespeare and Company when I was on a year abroad—every single book was gone.

Where all my books had been were copies of *Pride and Prejudice,* a novel I do not love. Jane Austen is alright, but I had told the kids that I would never be one of those middle-aged women with a "I'd Rather Be reading Jane Austen" bumper sticker on my car. Now Jane

Austen novels were piled on my desk, and lining the window sill. I opened my closet to hang up my coat, and there they were again, on the shelf. One was even left open on my desk, with a pencil laid casually on it, as if I'd been annotating and then was interrupted. In the margin, a boyish hand had scrawled, "Brilliant!"

This was a very clever little stunt, admirable, really, and it required a comparable retribution. Because I had to get this kid, people. My rep was on the line. He was Moriarty to my Sherlock. So I thought about it for a couple of nights, then it came to me. And yes, it was elementary.

"Mrs. Wentworth? This is Maura Danner, Zach's English teacher. Do you have a minute?"

Of course, I had to check it out with Zach's mom. And she was gung-ho. In fact, when she heard what I intended to do, she came up with an even more outrageous plan than my own. Her plan involved disassembling his bed and moving it the basement, and although I loved her enthusiasm—turns out he'd been driving her nuts, too-- moving heavy furniture was too much work on my part. No, I assured her, I had a much more diabolical idea.

"Zach is working at a restaurant on the weekend, right?"

"Yes, he works until midnight on

Saturday."

"What does he do when he gets off work? You know, to unwind?"

"Well, let's see. he comes home and takes a shower, then he usually plays guitar for a while before he goes to bed..."

Bingo.

Now all I had to do was wait, let him get cocky, thinking he'd won.

So I waited three weeks, then I went to Zach's house and his mom showed me into his creepy adolescent boy room and there it was, in the corner: his guitar. I took it, and I put a small envelope on his computer keyboard, where he was sure to see it. His mom agreed not to say a word about helping me, we had a glass of wine and a very satisfying giggle, and I left.

The next day I did not have Zachary's class, but his mom called me to tell me with glee that indeed Zachary had come home all sweaty and tired, took a shower, and went to play his guitar. He found my note instead and went berserk: "Was she in my room? HOW DID SHE GET IN MY ROOM?!" You see, as horrified as we teachers are that the kids will discover our personal lives and glean from it our weaknesses, what a kid fears most is his teacher touching all his personal crap and finding out that eew, he likes *In Sync*? An eye for an eye.

I held the guitar hostage until all my books were replaced, and that kid never bothered me again. The story of Danner's Revenge went viral, and now the other kids looked at me with new respect. They didn't know that Zach's mom had been in on it, so to them this was legitimate B & E. Their teacher was officially a badass. You mess with Danner, she will steal your guitar. From your *room*.

Of course, being an English teacher, I like to think that it was my note that scared the piss out of Zachary Wentworth. It was only one line, but one line of Oscar Wilde is all you need: *Revenge is a dish best served cold.*

Get Over Yourself

You've heard of the Sage on Stage, right? You know, the teacher who strolls around the room, pausing dramatically at the board until the whole class settles down and focuses on him, so he can deliver his brilliance uninterrupted? This guy loves to recite, always finds an excuse to read his own short-story-in-progress to the class, and spends a lot of time behind the lectern. Here's a hot tip for ya: Get over yourself.

You are older than your students, yes. You are more experienced, yes. You are presumably better read, because you have lived a longer life and have frittered more of it away in the tub with a novel. This does not make you superior. Well, it actually *does* make you superior, because of course you know more than they do, but it does not make you Dorothy Parker at the Round Table, guzzling gin and dazzling kids with your pithy wit. OK, OK, in your *mind* you are Dorothy Parker, but to your students—even to They Who Admire You—you are a middle-aged spinster obsessed with crap no one cares about anymore.

I'm talking about making a fool of yourself. Someday, probably when you're still green, some kid is going to test your ego, and the sooner you pass the test and move on to humbler pastures, the better teacher you'll be.

The kid's name was Evan Morell.

He was only an average student, but in person Evan was very impressive.

He reminded me of guys I'd worked with on my college newspaper, smart and sarcastic. He used to hang around my room during lunch, his skinny legs swinging down from the desk he was sitting on, and ask for my opinion about all sorts of goofy things: Did I think Mr. Keller was really a bionic man? (No.) Did I think it was better to be feared, or loved? (Feared, of course.) Did I think that man would ever invent a decent frozen pizza? (Maybe, if it were invented by an Italian.) Who did I think was the better writer, Tolkien or Lewis? (Lewis, hands down.) What was my position on free will? (Dostoevsky.)

Evan sought my opinion and he listened to it, which was flattering, since no one else did. He remembered things I said casually in class, he got my jokes. He had wit and cleverness that elevated our discussions, and I bantered with him a lot. He made me feel like a great teacher, because here was this wonderful student, being witty all over my room. He could hang out anywhere, all the teachers liked him, but he chose my room. This, I mistakenly thought, was the mark of a great teacher.

A few weeks of this go by, and I am feeling pretty good about myself. I seem to be possessed of a clarity of thought that astounds me. I dredge up facts and terminology I didn't know I knew. My head is humming with ideas that float and neatly lock into each other with a tidy little click as we move through the text. I have popped a Benadryl for my hay fever and had a triple cappuccino and I suddenly love everything these kids say. No one is stupid today. Even Earl is content to sit and study lyrics from *A Night at The Opera* with his monocle, occasionally checking in with reality to see if it's still there. By noon I am certain that there is no better feeling than this. When everyone is reading *Hamlet* and we're all getting it the same way and there are lovely pauses full of reverence, punctuated by Evan saying, "Damn, this guy is good." He has spoken for all of us, and I smile at him without intention, a smug expression on my face that must make me look like a clown on ecstasy, but I don't care.

There is a physical energy in the room as well. It's choreography, the way I perch on the table in the middle of the room, then swoop over to Audrey's desk and lean over for effect, saying very slowly, believing my own beautiful words,

"You know, Audrey, all the really great books are about time." Today for the first time I don't feel like a fake. I have abandoned the script, I've chucked the lesson plan and I am cooking without a recipe, dancing without steps, teaching by instinct. So this is why people do it, I think. This feeling of trusting yourself because you know the book better than you know yourself, and you can make it dance. I am *inspired*.

We talk about time for a few minutes, and Hamlet's place in it. We're chucking around terms that don't really mean anything, but they feel good. The kids are actually tasting their first really intense literary talk, and they like it. Anton, a chubby kid in the back, makes a remote but interesting link between Yeats's *The Second Coming* and Act II. Evan thinks this is a weak hypothesis, and he shoots Anton down, but he does it like a prince, with dignity, so Anton feels that he is Evan's equal. I don't have to do much here, I could actually leave the room and they would keep on talking about *Hamlet*. Evan could take my place. He is that good. I have *made* him that good. I am the best teacher in the whole school, and this class right here, right now, is the proof. I bet Laverdiere is downstairs nominating me for Teacher of The Year right this instant. After six months of teaching, I have bagged the peak and now I will become an educational consultant with my own teacher talk show where I deliver advice to well-intentioned but inept young teachers. I will write a teacher book and Oprah will read it and I will be on the show. She will ask me to co-host a special on teachers and I will say yes, if she throws in the house in Hawaii.

The next morning before the bell rings, Evan stands in front of my door holding a single rose. My heart flutters—my god, the boy has a little crush on me, I think, and I decide to let him down gently. I open the door and we walk into the room. I grab a small vase and stick the flower in it, but Evan doesn't comment on it. He's too eager to get to his question of the day. As I settle in at my desk, Evan takes his perch again on the desk, and starts in.

"What do you think about *Ode on a Grecian Urn*?"

Once again, I am thrilled that a) someone gives a rat's tuckus about what I think; and b) that the poem he is asking about is a damned good one; and c) that I have just finished reading it with another class and I can rattle off entire stanzas, which is damned impressive.

"What do you mean what do I think?" I practically yell. "I think it's fantastic. I love what it says."

"And what do you think it says?" he asks

smoothly, leaning back on his hands.

I swivel around in my teacher chair and chew on my pencil, feeling as luxurious as a patient on a psychiatrist's couch. This is all about me. I am the center. I can let fly, so I do. I deliver what sounds to me as I am saying it a brilliant assessment of the poem's essential thrust, that art expresses something about the human experience that only the artist can express; that poetry captures the ineffable, the sublime and the beautiful in life; the stuff we know is there but we can't get at except through art. While I'm at it, I offer an amusing anecdote about how I looked up the poem on the internet and found a Yale student's complete misread of it, based on a grammatical misstep in the third stanza.

"The reader thought the verb 'to be' was implied after 'human passion'. You know, like it was an elliptic phrase, which would negate the relative pronoun 'that' and therefore nullify the modifier that comes after it. So, I mean, it's ridiculous, but the guy actually thought that Keats was saying that human passion is far above the passion depicted on the urn, when in fact it's the opposite. the inverted subject and complement is misleading, but the better reader would have seen it."

Evan doesn't even blink when I spill all this. He knows what I am talking about. "Yeah, I can see that. The meaning, especially in these classical poems, is all in the structure. So you think Keats is saying..."

"I think he's saying that art is transcendent," I interrupt. I look at the clock. It's 7:38 am, and this conversation is what's transcendent, baby. It is the morning conversation of my dreams. I am discussing Keats with someone who gives a damn! I am amazing! He worships me!

"So why do you want to know about Keats?" I ask.

A shadowy smile flits across his mouth. "I'm presenting it in Enniger's class first period," he says. "We all have to explicate a poem with a classical theme."

Time screeches to a halt, backs up and stands idling, its foul exhaust on the air.

"And let me guess," I put it together slowly. "you're not prepared." That was typical Evan Morell, I thought, to rely on his wits when the stakes were high. I suddenly remember that he is really a B student, and a lazy one at that. That rose is looking pretty spent, I notice, and is the exact shade of the roses on the secretary's desk in the front office.

"I am now," he says, grinning. In the time it takes for him to hoist his stupid backpack onto his bony shoulders I understand that I have been had. I can feel my head puffing up into a bulbous shape and I feel a stutter coming on. I am Elmer Fudd, completely played by Bugs Bunny. I want to yell at him, but that would require me to admit that I had expected something of him—idolatry— that was completely inappropriate for me to expect.

For the rest of the day I hide out, licking my wounds, but by four-o'clock my mortification is just a weariness and a dull throbbing in my ribs. I have to hand it to the kid, I think. He worked me over like a conman. And my absurdly inflated opinion of myself has finally fizzled out. It was cruel, but he's a kid and kids are cruel, and you know, I don't think there was any other way.

Reading Lolita in a Trailer

A colleague of mine was once accused of forcing her students to reenact a rape in class. What she actually did was ask them to choose a scene from the novel and prepare it as a dramatic reading, and one kid chose the scene where the child protagonist is raped. A parent got wind of that and for the next six months the teacher was constantly in meetings with lawyers and administrators. So if you've read the novel, you're thinking, "But the whole point of the novel is the triumph over abuse!" True, but that's not the point. She'd been teaching *I Know Why the Caged Bird Sings*, one of the most challenged books in the high school canon, and conservative parents didn't want it there. They couldn't afford to send junior to a parochial school and they couldn't stand the secular curriculum, so they went after the teacher.

The same parents also objected to *Snow Falling on Cedars* (not enough foliage in the sex-in-the-tree scene). We also had one parent refuse to let his child read *Huckleberry Finn,* not because of the ubiquitous "N" word, but because Huck was a middle-school drop out. This was as bizarre as when a parent called me, outraged that I would teach a book entitled *Catch Her in the Raw.* It would have been hilarious except that one of my students would have been denied the experience of a lifetime: reading Salinger for the first time at fifteen. And I happen to be in the business of providing those kinds of experiences.

The trouble is, really conservative parents don't want *any* of the books you're going to want to teach to be there. You see the book as a stunning piece of art that your students will be better off for knowing, and parents see it as part of a slippery slope to a complete lack of standards and the decline of the Republic.

Shockingly to me, I went the Parents Against Bad Books in Schools website and found that all the books I taught were on the hit list. Every single one! The dirty words, suggestive phrases and mature content had been pulled out of context and listed nakedly on the screen, and that was the extent of the analysis. Curiously, not a single Bad Parent Against Great Books objected to the pedestrian *Chicken Soup for the Teenage Soul.* What could be worse for young minds than the glorification of mediocrity? I wondered. Clearly the question of literary merit was not on the table.

My colleague weathered the storm and

went on teaching what she thought made good academic sense, but she was constantly heckled. Me, I shut my door and prayed that no one would notice that I, too, had invited controversy into the classroom. I was lucky; so far no one had complained about Tim O'Brien's obscenely violent and explicit novel about Vietnam, *The Things They Carried*, nor had anyone protested against the word "motherfucker" appearing three times in T.C. Boyle's story *Greasy Lake,* which I'd read out loud. (It's meant to be hilarious, and it is.)

Then my students asked me when I was going to do *Lolita* in my after-school book discussion group.

I'd first read *Lolita* at age fifteen, when my brother, who had already gone through his own Nabokov stage and had moved on to Tolstoy, threw it on my bed and said, "Read this. You'll like it." I read it carelessly, and I still thought it the most magnificent world I had ever entered. I understood nothing—I was merely soaking in the language and the atmosphere. I don't think I really comprehended the plot (psychotic pedophile seduces and kidnaps girl child/love object and traipses around the country with her until the jig is up and he kills her phantom lover and winds up in prison writing a book) and I understood even less the psychological complexities of the main character (his sexual delicacy; his refined, pre-war European sensibilities; his painstakingly literary mind; his voracious malevolence and exquisite courtesy), but I loved every blessed page.

It was a book that wanted more of me than I could give, and I was ready for a book to ask that of me. Each page exhausted me—not necessarily because of its erudition and the scholarly expectations it had of its reader, but because of its vitality. *Lolita* was more alive than any other book I had read. When I finished the last page, I actually shivered.

I'd been talking about reading *Lolita* for some time, and now my students were, in their own way, telling me that they were ready for a book to ask more of them than they could give. My juniors had begun with Nabokov's essay, "Good Readers and Good Writers". We had been talking about the act of reading all year long, and I had asked my students to pay attention to how they read and *why* they read. We frequently referred to Nabokov's analogy of the panting reader working hard to ascend the mountain and being rewarded with an authorial embrace at the top, and the kids loved this notion that a good book should demand something of them. They were bored with the passivity of the easy read, and the cliche of the politically correct novel. Barely formed themselves, they were ready to be transformed by a book.

The previous selection for my after-school literary group had been the charming grammar expose, *Eats, Shoots, and Leaves*, and only one myopic kid had shown up. We had a breathtaking discussion about the history of the apostrophe, but I needed something more meaty. So in between classes I fired off a cheery e-mail to Laverdiere, to let him know that the next book would indeed be *Lolita*.

His reply was speedy. "Hold off on this—we need to discuss this first," he wrote, which is Principal for "Holy Shit! I might actually have to get a backbone!"

"Ok, let's talk after school," I typed back. Then I cancelled the announcements for the book and trembled with rage for the rest of the afternoon, suspecting that Laverdiere was going to put the kibosh on my literary lust. He and I had discussed the possibility of reading *Lolita* a while back, in the midst of the parental fury over my colleague's alleged rape assignment, and he had suggested in passing that it might be a good idea to have parents sign a paper of "acknowledgement" before their children participated in that particular discussion. I knew that he was doing his job—trying to preempt, diffuse, and appease without caving. I had ignored this at the time, but now I would have to come clean and tell him that I couldn't do that because it was against my principles. (Pesky thing, principles. So much easier to teach if you have none.) I am always willing to discuss anything I teach, but to treat *Lolita* with apologetic guilt felt disrespectful. By the last period of the day I knew that I could not compromise on this issue without feeling compromised myself. The book discussion group would dissolve into the air, I imagined, because no one else wanted to take it on and I would refuse to if I couldn't do *Lolita*.

When I went to see Laverdiere after school, he wasn't there, so I had another night to cool down and think about it. *Was* there any reason not to read *Lolita* with high school kids? I considered:

1. The language. Well, yes, in places it probably could be considered obscene, if the reader has taken advanced French and knows the crude little meaning of "vermeillette fente". Otherwise not a single expletive.

2. The immoral subject matter. After channel surfing for five seconds and alighting on the lurid image of a bikini-sporting, buxom bimbette chugging a blender full of maggots (good old Fear Factor), I concluded that the

secret sexual longings of a middle aged European man for a lovely young girl were positively Disney. And surely Hester Prynne's fatally arrogant statement to her minister-lover, "What we did had a consecration of its own," was more appalling than Humbert's open admission that he was indeed a monster. So if I didn't do *Lolita* maybe I should stop teaching *The Scarlet Letter.*

3. My ego. I tossed this one around for quite a while. Was I just being provocative, secretly hoping that kids would want to read the book because they knew the film was racy and had even been banned (the Jeremy Irons one, not the James Mason one, which they would ignore because it is in black and white)? Did I *want* parents to come rattling their dictionaries of archaic French at my door, fuming because they sure as hell knew the meaning of "vermeillette fente," thank you very much, and I couldn't pull the wool over their eyes? No, I definitely did not want that kind of attention. No teacher does.

The next day I braced myself for The Talk with The Principal. I got to work early and was just about to go into his office when I looked up and saw on the giant TV screen that parades our daily announcements a hot-pink backdrop with salacious script advertising *Lolita* as the next Book Talk selection, complete with those valentine sunglasses, that sticky red mouth and the fellatiative (don't bother looking it up, I invented it) lollypop.

Who was the villain who had disobeyed my explicit message NOT to proceed with the *Lolita* announcement until I had the go-ahead from Laverdiere? I wanted to write the copy myself, knowing that this kind of cheap shot would be some lay person's attempt at getting kids excited about reading it. It was exactly the wrong way to go. Besides, in the book Lo doesn't wear red, heart-shaped glasses. She wears "stern dark spectacles," and there is no lollypop.

"Where is Greg?" I demanded as I blew into the library. School had not yet started; there was still a chance that I might not be fired if I could find the A.V. guy and wring his neck before the bell rang. The assistant librarian looked up from her desk.

"He's in the back," she said, with the neutral expression of a good bartender.

Just then Guilty Greg appeared, a lascivious grin on his face. "Hey, 'bout time you read something a little more exciting than that grammar crap," he said.

"Get it off right now," I answered tersely. "You weren't supposed to run anything until I wrote the copy myself."

"Oops. Sorry," he said, and he scuttled off

to fix it.

A thought burst behind my pinpoint eyes.

"Have you even *read* it?" I called after him.

"No," he said, disappearing into the A.V. room.

I turned to the assistant librarian, who was slinking behind her desk.

"Have you read it?" I accused.

"Nope."

When I finally went into Laverdiere"s office that afternoon, he took one look at me and put his head down on the desk. For a moment I thought he was having a thrombosis, but his shoulders were hunching with hilarity and he lifted his head up and smiled.

"Of all the books in the world, why *Lolita?*" he said. He'd been through the ringer, and didn't want to go through it again if he didn't have to. I explained that the reason I wanted to do *Lolita* was because the book was simply too wonderful to pass up. Because I knew and loved it, because I was willing to explore it with less experienced readers, because it could show the modern American reader an older, European world of ideas, and because I wanted to inspire kids to read something intellectually challenging.

While he was, understandably, worried about parents storming his office in protest, the biggest risk in my mind, I told him, was not the book's raciness. The risk was that it would be too intense for a non-required read. After all this, what if no one came because the book was too hard? What if we couldn't even *have* the conversation about whether or not the book deserved to be called a classic? This, I said, would be the real horror. This, Laverdiere said with a sigh, would be a relief.

"Ok, go ahead, but you're on your own with it," was his final word.

"You've read it, right?" I said casually as I got up to leave.

"Not for years."

I took that as a "no."

The next day there was a newspaper on my desk. I never did find out who put it there. The headline on the front page of the Portland Press Herald read: *Teen's Mom Rekindles Debate Over Novel: The Controversial Catcher in the Rye Shouldn't be Taught to Ninth-graders.* (True—ninth graders are generally goobers.) I decided to talk about this with my juniors who had just finished reading the novel with me. The woman in the article had made her pronouncement that the book was immoral before she had read it, I explained to them, quoting the paper, and I asked them what they thought of that. No fools, they, my students scoffed at the woman's "researching" the book in Sparknotes. ("She didn't even use the *real* Spark notes," Audrey said. "She went to Sparknotes.com.") Then we read a little bit of the book, and went back to the article. "Anyone see anything immoral here?" I asked. "Anyone see any reason not to read this book?" Cora mentioned the use of "goddamn," and we agreed that to some people with particular religious feelings this could be offensive. The woman in the article had cited "prostitutes" and "promiscuous sex" as objectionable content, and someone said that Jesus had slept with a prostitute, so we shouldn't read the Bible, either. Someone else, staying closer to the text, recalled that promiscuous sex was hardly Holden's problem. We agreed that the book was wasted on freshmen, that it was better to read it as a junior, because Holden is a junior and sixteen year olds are considerably more mature than fourteen year olds. I was comforted by their sound reasoning. They had confidence because they had actually read the book, deeply, and they spoke with the authority of their own life experiences. This, I thought, boded well for *Lolita*. Students would not be shocked by the story, nor would they be corrupted by its dubious "values," if indeed it expresses any. And the word "goddamn" does not appear.

226

That night my friend Suki stopped by and casually mentioned that she was reading *Lolita* with her book group. "Oh yeah?" I said, perking up. "How's it going?"

"Well, one person said she wouldn't read it because it felt too much like soft porn."

"Really? Someone said that?"

"Yeah, I guess it made her uncomfortable."

"What's wrong with soft porn?" I said, and we laughed.

Late that night the headline, *Teacher Peddles Soft Porn to Students,* floated into mental view. I knew the parts Suki''s friend was thinking of, and they are unutterably sexy. Yet even when Nabokov is explicit, he is original, and the language is intoxicating, not vulgar. Does the reader feel the tingle of a sexual current? Hell, yes. And when Lady Macbeth says, "Come, you spirits that tend on mortal thoughts, unsex me here," doesn't every kid in the room squirm a little? Great writers write about things that matter, and sexual longing matters. Good readers encounter sexy passages, acknowledge that yes, we are all susceptible to lust, and lust feels great, and then they move on to other aspects of the book. The weak reader is immobilized by a graphic image and cannot move on. In all my years of teaching in public schools, I have never seen a student who was a weak reader in this sense. I have seen a few parents who were weak readers, but never has a kid been unable to understand or enjoy a novel because of a sexy scene or a profane word. They think about it, smile or wonder (depending on their own experience), and move on.

So the fateful day arrived. It was two twenty. In ten minutes the book talk was supposed to begin. I felt like I was twenty and having my first dinner party. Would anyone come? What if only two kids showed up and they hated each other? (This actually happened at my first dinner party.) What if there was so much intellectual disparity that it was impossible to manage a balanced discussion? Worse, what if the book really was too hard for high school readers to plow through on their own? Maybe this was a stupid idea.

At two twenty-four Hannah came in and threw her book bag down on a chair and I wanted to hug her. She quickly confessed that she hadn't finished the book, she was only half way through. I assured her that she could still bring something to the discussion. Mallory, who had done a thirty-minute presentation on Nabokov's story "Spring in Fialta" the month before, swaggered in. Her hair was usually blue, and I noticed with surprise that today it was merely glossy brown. Next came Ben, who resembled an Afghan puppy and was an excellent reader. He slumped down on a desk in the back and announced that he was nearly moved to tears when Humbert was leaving Lolita forever, and I got the first tingle of the good stuff to come. Emily, the last one here by two thirty, was my ballerina. When she got intimate with a book she didn't like to give away her thoughts, but today she was bubbling over. "I *love* this book," she said.

We started right in, tossing around our general reactions to the novel when Tom, dressed in a zoot suit and spats, came in quietly and took a seat next to Hannah.

"We're right at the juicy part," I said. "We're talking about whether or not Lolita seduces Humbert." They had intuitively gravitated toward one of the central paradoxes of the book: Lolita has sexual experience (she is not a virgin when she has sex with her stepfather), but she does not know the implications of her actions.

Hannah pointed out that Humbert tells the reader outright that Lolita seduced *him*.

"Yeah, but that's just him being an unreliable narrator," argued Ben.

We then made a connection between

Nabokov's narrators and those of Poe, in particular the narrator from *The Fall of the House of Usher*. Mallory admitted that she liked Humbert, even though she knew he was despicable. We quickly agreed that we sympathized with his suffering, that Nabokov was artful in his manipulation of the reader's emotions. I had put a quote on the board about Nabokov's idea that fiction is a "game of worlds" and we talked about the idea of the reader being pitted against the author in an elaborate web of allusion and double meaning. "You have to read through this guy's version of the story, just like you have to see through Holden Caulfield's cynicism to get that the story is really all about his brother's death," Emily observed. Reading through the narrator's voice to see the author's purpose is something we'd worked on, and I was pleased that she could do this.

"Oh!" Hannah had a sudden insight. She smiled shyly when we looked at her. "I just got that the guy in the red car is Quilty. Cool." This started us on the subject of Quilty, and someone trotted out the term "doppelganger". We hashed out the idea of alter egos, those shadowy selves that reveal dark purposes, like Humbert's Quilty-that-sounds-like-Guilty, a child pornographer and hack playwright who pursues Humbert and Lolita across the country. It was here that Tom offered his one comment for the whole discussion: "Humbert is not really in love with Lolita, he's in love with art." I could tell that the kids didn't know exactly what he meant, but they nodded in acceptance. Tom was a cult figure in the school, an icon in 1940s clothes who did not need to be explained. So we just kept going.

"What I love is how Lolita totally deflates Humbert, like when they're in the hospital and she tells him to cut out the French," said Ben, who had now crawled over the desks into the front row so his legs could spread out.

"Yeah, Lolita definitely has the best lines," Mallory agreed.

This nudged the conversation toward the ocean that separates Lolita's dialog from Humbert's. I was the only one with an annotated copy of the book, and I trod carefully, not wanting to have all the answers before they got to play. I let them bang around this topic for a while, then I proposed that Lolita seemed to be the America of the fifties—slangy, irreverent, indifferent to the past, and Humbert was like the dead Old World. The novel, I said, depicted the tug of America on the immigrant imagination, the seduction of the philistine society. They stared at me. This was not a class and I had not prepared notes or discussion questions. I was winging it, and they knew this, and this put me on their level. For a moment I remembered what it was like to be fifteen again, tossing out a half-baked theory in a room of smart people.

"Cool," murmured Hannah, and we kept moving.

It was now almost four o'clock and the conversation was winding down. "So what line really got to you?" I asked.

"When Humbert says at the end, 'I'll die if you touch me,'" Emily immediately said. We women concurred that there was a nauseating pathos in those words—Humbert is so desperate and eighteen-year-old, pregnant, married Lolita is so oblivious to his pain—but Ben saw it differently.

"I have no sympathy for the guy. No way. What really gets me is when Lolita comes into his bed after she finds out her mother is dead and Humbert says 'You see, she had absolutely no where else to go.'" He was right, the line resonated and we were quiet for a while, reverent in the face of Ben's sensitivity. Ben, we were suddenly certain, was a good man.

We ended by talking about stolen childhood and ruined lives, then we made a tentative plan to read *Middlesex* for the next selection. Jeffrey Eugenides' Pulitzer-prize winning novel about a hermaphrodite is beautiful and haunting and full of things to talk about, but it also has sexually explicit scenes and plenty of bad language. I made a mental note to warn Laverdiere so he wouldn't have a real thrombosis, but this time I didn't need to soul search. As I walked across the parking lot I experienced a teaching peace of mind, a knowledge that the lesson had gone well. The feeling was ephemeral, like Nabokov's butterflies, for there would be failures tomorrow. Nonetheless, I was satisfied for the moment, convinced that my students were not in danger. They were not delicate creatures, impotent in the face of challenging, controversial or even disturbing texts. Left alone with a good book, they could find their way through the pitfalls of petty interpretation to a deeper, better read.

Teach the best books you can. Don't ever stop doing that, no matter what anyone says.

Lilacs on the Desk: It's Time

I'm running out of steam here, and I think I've told you most of what you need to know, or at least what I can teach you. The rest you'll have to figure out by yourself.

One thing you need to be ready for, though, is how to let go. Your first year is intense, and after a few short months that rocket past, the kids you have come to adore are going to leave you. Because you are so young, you have given them your soul, and because they are so young, they are ungrateful: they are going to graduate. If you're lucky, they won't come back. It's horrible when they come back. They stand around while you interview them about their new grown up lives (How was university? Where are you living now? What are you doing? Grad school?) and they never ask you about yours, because *they're not your freaking friends*. So anything you might tell an actual *friend* is off limits. They don't want you to be their friend anyway—they want you to be proud of them. Your job is to tell them that yes, you are proud of them, then get someone to page you and say that you're urgently needed in a meeting. I usually arrange this with one of the secretaries. If they see an old student headed my way, they wait about ten minutes then the P.A says "Ms. Danner to the front office, please." Believe me, it's better this way. The kids you really love, that you really cannot live without yet somehow you must—they don't ever come back. Somehow they know not to.

The kids feel it, too, the leaving. Especially the seniors. They won't sing "To Sir with Love" or anything, but they hang around after school. They'll pick a day when it's pretty quiet, and you just happen to be in your room, working late. They may not know it, but they're trying to do what Holden Caulfield is trying to do at the beginning of *The Catcher in the Rye*. They are trying to feel some kind of a good-bye. Years from now they won't remember how they stood around your desk and watched it all die in the space of fifteen minutes one afternoon, but you will.

It's June, and it's late, almost 5:30, and Mallory comes by to see me. It's been a while, and I am surprised to see that her hair is shocking lime green today, and she looks lovely in it. No one can wear that bilious shade except Mallory. She walks into the room and plunks herself down in my reading chair. Mallory is a cat; she's at home everywhere. She is a vigorous writer, she won the state Writer of the Year award and had already gotten her first rejection from *The New Yorker.* She is everything I wish I could have been at her age. She lolls around, swinging her legs.

"Hey Mallory. Have you started *Anna Karenina* yet?" I ask. The trailer is swelteringly hot. I lean forward and brush against the lilacs on my desk. This sends a waft of velvet mauve into the air. This blossom is the freshest scent I have ever inhaled. It rips through the staleness of acoustic tile and fluorescent lights and for a moment, I am revived. "Once you get the Russian thing in your veins, nothing else satisfies," I warn her.

"I haven't gotten to it yet, but I will," she replies. She is being polite. She's never polite. Outrageous, challenging, passionate, intense, but never has she been particularly polite. She is preparing. Already it's different.

"Well you are going to just LOVE it," I say.

I never say that.

Just then Zachary strolls into the room and Mallory looks at him the way the cat looks at the dog. He does not acknowledge her. He leans on my desk for a second and starts to touch my stapler.

"Zachary."

"Sorry. I just wanted to thank you. For

writing me that recommendation," he says shyly. Wow. So he does have a soul.

"That pack of lies? No problem," I answer, hiding the fact that I am touched. Mallory is still staring at him.

"Where are you going?" she asks him. I do believe this is the first exchange they have ever had.

"Greenfield Community," he answers boldly. He's proud of that, and he should be. He has spent the year slogging through the books, getting C's and D's from me, secretly petrified that when June comes around everyone else will be going somewhere except him. He knows that Mallory is probably off to some rich kid school where she will begin her fantastically privileged life of great food and good conversation and a stimulating career, and he's decided he doesn't care. What he doesn't know is that she's off to Stanford on a full scholarship, a place that would impress even this new, more self-assured Zachary. I wait for it—the Mallory I know will pounce then play with her prey. She will eviscerate him with her vocabulary, her beauty, and her own glaring ambitions.

Instead, she smiles and says, "Cool."

Zach nods, and there's a little moment between them, then, because he is named Zachary and therefore ADD up the wazoo, he slaps his hands on his thigh and says, "I gotta go. Thanks for a great year, Ms. Danner!" and he quick-steps out of my room. This is the first time a student has thanked me for teaching him, and I am stunned. All I can do is sit at my desk and look at the clock. It's what I do when something moves me and I don't want to show it. I have learned this from them, I think. I've learned all sorts of things from them that will probably take decades to sort out. I suddenly realize that I am not the person I was in September.

"So." Mallory finally says.

"So." I answer.

"You still have that poem?"

"Yep," I say. "I have it right here, on my desk. See?" She stands up and walks over to my desk and sees a little white paper with her beautiful words on it scotch-taped to my desk. It's an excellent poem, stark and perfect. It's better than most of the stuff I read in *The New Yorker.*

"You gonna send this one in?" I ask her.

"Yeah. Probably." Oh my God I love this kid—she is so brave and I am so proud of her for having the guts to wear lime green hair and write so honestly and be so fucking optimistic that she will just casually send in her poems to *The New Yorker.* She's got it, I think. She's got it and she doesn't know it, which is good. I can suddenly imagine the two of us having lunch in the Village someday, me making a toast at her wedding, sending a baby present to the happy couple, but it fades before I even see it clearly enough.

"Remember to write that book about the English teacher," I tease her.

She laughs and starts heading for the door.

"Ok," she says.

"And make her really smart and give her great clothes."

"Yeah, yeah. Ok."

And then she's gone.

I look at the clock. "Read *Anna Karenina*," I call out to the air.

"I will," she calls back from somewhere else.

I stare at the door, suspecting in my chilly, didactic heart that she will walk through galaxies of doors in her glittering promise of a life, but she will never walk through mine again. And I know that like the last page of some enchanting book that hints at all the unseen, unread wonders to come, my chapter with her is done.

Last Word

So that's it. I'm lightin' out for the territories. I'm turning in my letter tomorrow, which is the absolute last day of the teaching year so no one can arrange for me to receive a rocking chair, or a gift certificate to LL Bean, a bench, a plaque or—Kiss Of Death—a bench with a plaque on it.

They say that it's easy to leave teaching on the last day of June. It's not going back on the first day of September that's hard. Actually, I don't know what I'll do when I wake up and don't have to think about Amanda's 504—that might free up some serious mental space. I always thought that after teaching I'd take off for Europe and become a cabaret singer, but I can't sing and I'm not even going to tell you what your pension is going to be when you retire, but it doesn't exactly support a Paris apartment. Maybe Charles and I will go back to New York and live under Claire's bed. Maybe Charles will quit his job and we'll be one of those old couples who ride motorcycles across the country; I've always wanted a Harley. Or I could raise miniature dachshunds, like my old high school French teacher. Who knows?

I'm sure leaving the classroom for good

240

will be tough, but somehow knowing that you are in the game now makes it alright. Writing this book has helped me come away from the edge of the cliff, and I can let it go.

People, the bell's about to ring.

Now go teach. Go teach like hell.

Made in the USA
Columbia, SC
21 October 2017